WITH JESUS

—— IN THE ——

UPPER ROOM

WITH *Jesus*

—— IN THE ——

UPPER ROOM

·DAVID WINTER·

FORTY GOSPEL REFLECTIONS FROM JOHN 13—17

Text copyright © David Winter 2002
The author asserts the moral right
to be identified as the author of this work

Published by
The Bible Reading Fellowship
First Floor, Elsfield Hall
15–17 Elsfield Way, Oxford OX2 8FG
ISBN 1 84101 324 2

First published 2001
This edition 2002
1 3 5 7 9 10 8 6 4 2 0
All rights reserved

Acknowledgments

Unless otherwise stated, scripture quotations are taken from
The New Revised Standard Version of the Bible, Anglicized Edition,
copyright © 1989, 1995 by the Division of Christian Education of
the National Council of the Churches of Christ in the USA, and are
used by permission. All rights reserved.

Scripture quotations taken from the Holy Bible, New International
Version, copyright © 1973, 1978, 1984 by International Bible
Society, are used by permission of Hodder & Stoughton Limited.
All rights reserved. 'NIV' is a registered trademark of International
Bible Society. UK trademark number 1448790.

Scriptures quoted from the Good News Bible published by The Bible
Societies/HarperCollins Publishers Ltd, UK © American Bible Society
1966, 1971, 1976, 1992, used with permission.

Extracts from the Authorized Version of the Bible (The King James
Bible), the rights in which are vested in the Crown, are reproduced
by permission of the Crown's patentee, Cambridge University Press.

A catalogue record for this book is available from the British Library

Printed and bound in Great Britain by
Omnia Books Limited, Glasgow

CONTENTS

READING JOHN'S GOSPEL

This book invites the reader to spend forty days reflecting on five chapters of John's Gospel, those which contain the so-called 'upper room discourses'. It is not a commentary, much less a work of biblical scholarship, but rather a close devotional study of perhaps the most cherished part of a deeply cherished Gospel.

John's Gospel does not always make for simple reading. It demands something of the reader—time, certainly, space to reflect, and a spiritual imagination to look beyond the surface to the deeper truths that lie in these familiar words and phrases. All of those disciplines, of course, can be associated with Lenten reflection, and my hope and prayer is that this book will be a help to the reader on that forty-day journey from Ash Wednesday to the glory of Easter morning. (If you are using the book for Lenten study, you need to note that the forty days cover Mondays to Saturdays only.)

As soon as we turn to this Gospel, we are aware of being in a different environment from the other three—Matthew, Mark and Luke. The blunt rabbi Jesus, with his stories and pithy sayings, seems to have been transformed into something of a philosopher, who teases out a profound meaning from such apparently ordinary ideas as birth, blindness, light and darkness. He performs miracles, but the writer never calls them that: they are 'signs'—clues, evidences, keys to understanding.

Most people reading this Gospel are struck by the feeling that all the while there's 'more to this than meets the eye'. And there is! That's one of the clues to appreciating John. Every story, every discourse, every event seems to be capable of interpretation at several levels. Perhaps that's why, from the very earliest days of the Church, this Gospel has been so popular with preachers.

In fact, the story the Gospel tells is essentially the same as the others. But it has the feel of 'emotion recollected in tranquillity', as Wordsworth defined poetry. These are the events and words of the life of Jesus recollected and filtered through the long experience of one who was an eye-witness of what occurred but had time also to see and evaluate its impact on the believing community that those events brought into existence.

So it is pointless to ask—as any reader is tempted to do—'Are these the actual words of Jesus? Is this a verbatim record of what he said on that Thursday evening long ago?' It is not less but more than that, for here is the *effect* of what was said, seen now in the light of what followed—the cross, the empty tomb, Pentecost and the birth of the new community. John's is a Gospel of profound vision, of truth beyond truth.

And of that truth this discourse is a kind of distillation. For forty days let's imagine ourselves sitting with those disciples as the darkness falls outside and the light among them grows brighter and brighter. Through the ears, eyes and memory of the 'beloved disciple' we may be able to share in the wonder of a quite extraordinary evening.

SETTING THE SCENE

It was April in the year 30 and Jerusalem was getting ready for the Passover. Already the pilgrims were making their way into the city from the provinces, and members of families were returning home to share in the feast. It had been an extraordinary week for the city, beginning with the arrival the previous Sunday of Jesus and his Galilean disciples, trooping down the Mount of Olives in a noisy demonstration of loyalty and affection, the prophet himself riding on an ass. This had been followed by a disturbance in the temple courts, when Jesus had forcibly ejected some squalid dealers in religious articles, and by a series of confrontations between him and the religious establishment.

But now that the feast was so near, something like calm was settling over the city. The disciples of Jesus had been sent on a strange, but apparently pre-planned, expedition to ensure that there was a suitable room for him and his followers to eat a meal together. It was to be in an 'upper room', a *katalouma*, a guest chamber provided by the anonymous 'owner of the house' (Mark 14:14). There the Twelve gathered with Jesus for an evening which would be unlike anything they had ever experienced before. Whether what took place then was in fact the Passover meal, the *seder*, as the other Gospels claim, or whether (as John 18:28 implies) that took place (according to normal custom) on the following day, and this was for Jesus and his friends a solemn meal with Passover characteristics but not the actual ceremony, we must leave to the disputes of the scholars. What is clear is that the occasion was imbued with a deep and unique significance by Jesus himself, who was only too well aware of what lay ahead for him before that year's Passover was over.

In that quiet room, gathered around the table, the disciples were to sit in amazement as their master drew back the veil that hides heaven from earth and the hidden purposes of God from human eyes. For the 'beloved disciple', who seems to be the source of this remarkable Gospel, these were words to treasure, to be captured in the memory by the Spirit. They would enlighten the hearts and minds of the disciples not only through the traumas of the next few days, but also until the day when each of them in his own way would discover their fulfilment in the kingdom of heaven. Beyond that, through this written recollection of that evening, millions of believers in Jesus in later ages would share something of their experience.

It can be said quite simply: there has never been teaching like this, because there has never been a teacher like Jesus. And it is this teaching, this upper room 'discourse', which is to be the material of this forty-day reflection.

These words have retained their power and wisdom. Still today they echo through the life of the Church—obedience, love, strength and joy. Their images are timeless—the branches of the vine, the fruit that it yields, the divine husbandman who prunes the dead wood. It is full of phrases that have entered into our language and culture far beyond the walls of our churches—'greater love', the 'new commandment', 'let not your hearts be troubled', 'love one another', 'my peace I give to you'. On a journey from Ash Wednesday to Easter Eve, there can be no better words to reflect on, to make our own and to illuminate the way.

For biblical scholars, this was a 'farewell discourse'. That's not quite the same as the 'last words' of Jesus, because those words were to be spoken from the cross—and, indeed, there would be words, vital words, spoken to his followers after the resurrection. But this 'discourse' (defined by the Oxford English Dictionary as 'a talk, lecture or sermon at length on a subject') was different, not only in its duration but in its intention. A 'farewell discourse' in the ancient world was an opportunity for a distinguished leader or teacher to explain to his followers how his work was to be continued after his departure—how the torch that he had lit was to be kept alight and passed on for the future. It was an opportunity not to look back, but to look ahead.

That is the hallmark of these upper room discourses, recalled and reflected on by one who was surely there (for this has all the marks of an eye-witness account). They have a spiritual—I almost wrote 'mystical'—quality about them which marks them out from almost anything else in the Bible. These are the recollections—probably long after the event—of someone who was privileged to sit at the feet of Jesus for one unforgettable evening while the curtains of eternity were rolled back and, for a while, the ways of God unfolded.

All four Gospels tell us of this upper room, but for the other three—the ones known as the 'synoptic' or 'one-eyed' Gospels, because they often speak with one voice—the centrepiece is the *seder* meal itself, with the institution of the Christian 'passover', the Lord's Supper. John's Gospel sees no need to report what was already known and indeed was part of the life and worship of all the churches. Here first place is given not to that dramatic presentation of the new covenant, sealed for ever in the crucified body and the shed blood of the Saviour, but to the equally dramatic lesson in humility that began that evening, and the unfolding of a new commandment, a new way of life and a new spiritual power which would be theirs after the impending events of the Passion were over.

This, Jesus was saying, is what it is *really* all about. This is why I came and this is why I am going. Here is the future, full of persecution and promise, full of confrontation and opposition, but also full of the divine 'Helper' who would be sent among them.

We can, if we wish, compare this discourse of Jesus with the final words of Moses, on the brink of the promised land (Deuteronomy 31—34), or with Jacob's farewell to his sons (Genesis 49). In the ancient world there are other examples: Socrates' farewell in Plato's *Phaedo* is probably the best-known example. But none can approach the sublimity of spiritual insight or breadth of vision that are to be found here. Time is almost put into suspense. The past, present and future seem to become one. Love, hope and glory are its great themes, all bound up in what lay ahead for Jesus and for these anxious disciples.

And there is rich promise, too. Another 'helper', a *parakletos*, one to stand alongside them in the future as Jesus had done in the past, would be his parting gift to his followers. The very elusiveness of the title—'advocate', say some modern translations; 'comforter', says the King James Version—is part of the mystery to be unfolded. This will be the 'Spirit of truth', a way in which the Father and the Son would continue to be with the new community, an abiding, constant and unfailing presence.

Again, there has never been a promise like this, because there has never been a gift like this one.

The narrative from chapters 13—17, which we shall be reflecting on in these pages, covers, it would seem, no more than a few hours, though it has taken two-and-a-half years of the ministry of Jesus to reach this point. Now, time stands still, as it were. So be it. These are timeless words. Forty days is a very short time to make them our own.

1

The full extent
of his love

Now before the festival of the Passover, Jesus knew that his hour had come to depart from this world and go to the Father. Having loved his own who were in the world, he loved them to the end. The devil had already put it into the heart of Judas son of Simon Iscariot to betray him. And during supper Jesus, knowing that the Father had given all things into his hands, and that he had come from God and was going to God, got up from the table, took off his outer robe, and tied a towel around himself. Then he poured water into a basin and began to wash the disciples' feet and to wipe them with the towel that was tied around him.

JOHN 13:1–5

Before the words, the action. All that Jesus was to say to them on this memorable evening was to be seen in the light of this, that he had washed their feet.

'Before the festival of the Passover' places the event in time, though not precisely. In the light of the other Gospel narratives, we may assume that this was the Thursday night before the Passover began with Sabbath at nightfall the next (Friday) evening. Again according to the other accounts, Thursday was the evening when Jesus shared the Passover meal, the *seder*, with his friends—probably, though not certainly, just 'the Twelve'.

First John puts the whole event into its wider—indeed,

eternal—perspective: 'Jesus knew that his hour had come to depart from this world and go to the Father.' This 'hour' had echoed through the Gospel: 'My hour has not yet come' (2:4); 'The hour has come for the Son of man to be glorified' (12:23). Now the hour was to be defined more precisely. It was the hour when Jesus would leave this world (that is, die) and return to his Father. As we shall see, that event would become his 'glorification'.

But the setting was even more profound than that. 'Jesus, knowing that the Father had given all things into his hands, and that he had come from God and was going to God'... did what? Announced his divine identity from the roof-tops? Invited their worship and honour? Asserted his authority over this collection of former fishermen, tax collectors and political activists? Far from it. He took upon himself the role of the servant waiting on them, put on an apron, filled a bowl with water and began to wash their feet. In that way the one who had come from God and was going back to God showed them what it meant to share the divine nature.

Presumably the disciples were waiting to see who was to perform this little courtesy of welcome, customary in an eastern home. There didn't appear to be a female or child slave present to undertake the menial task (normally too demeaning even for a male slave), nor a Gentile, it would seem—the next choice. Perhaps they looked at each other. All we have learnt of their attitude from the Gospels tells us that none of them would willingly volunteer for this lowly role. Hadn't they argued about who would be the greatest among them (Mark 9:34)? Hadn't two of them had the nerve to ask that the seats of honour at the right and left hand of Jesus should be theirs when he assumed kingly power (Mark 10:37)? To wash the others' feet would be a tacit admission of inferiority, and that was something they were extremely reluctant to accept.

So *Jesus did it*. By that action he put into practice his saying that the first shall be last and the last first (Mark 10:31) and that he who would be chief among them must become servant of all (Mark 10:44). By it also he spoke to all his followers down the ages. The disciples of Christ are not to stand on their dignity, insist on being treated with respect, fight for their 'rights'. That's why the squalid little struggles for power in church life are scandalous—not because they get in the local paper, or cause divisions in the congregation (though that is bad enough), but because they contradict the gospel itself.

I remember being shocked, as a student activist, at the way in which some of the left-wing 'comrades' with whom I associated would talk of the solidarity of the masses and so on, but fight with every means at their disposal to acquire power and leadership within the group. It was depressing, too, some time later, to find that same attitude in some who sought leadership in the Church.

So the simple example of Jesus should have taught his disciples—the ones around the table, and we who read about it now—an important lesson in humility and service. But he also showed them something more, something that is of priceless significance to all his disciples, then and now. He showed that he 'loved them *to the end*'. The 'end' here, in Greek, is *telos*, which literally means the closing act, the ultimate fulfilment. It is the root of the word that Jesus cried out in triumph from the cross, 'It is finished!'—the work the Father had given him to do had been completed. Now the word is applied to this act of loving and humble service. By it he revealed the full extent of his love for the disciples, and that his love for them would last 'to the end'. The love of Christ, in other words, is inexhaustible, without limit. It is the ultimate in both commitment and care. Washing their feet might have seemed to the disciples an un-dignified and menial way of serving. Jesus turned their values upside down, as he does with us too. This simple gesture demonstrated nothing less than the 'full extent' of his love for them. We should never underestimate the power of a loving act, however simple.

Those Jesus loved are described here as 'his own'. Perhaps our minds go back to the prologue of this Gospel, where we are told that Jesus came to 'his own', but his 'own' didn't receive him (1:11). There it refers to his own *people*, his kith and kin. Here he is referring to his 'new' people, those who *did* 'receive him' and through that became 'children of God' (1:12). With all their faults and failures to understand, he loved them 'to the end'. Thank God he still does.

There is one other word in this passage to note, because it is a verb that recurs time and again through the fourth Gospel—'knowing'. Jesus *knew* that his hour had come; he *knew* that the Father had given all things into his hands and he *knew* that he had come from God and was going to God. This 'knowledge' of the Messiah contrasts with the slowness of the disciples to understand, as we shall see later in these pages. Jesus' knowledge of these eternal truths was a measure of his divine nature—sharing, as it were, in the wisdom of God, a willing collaborator in his purposes.

The really staggering thought is that it was this bearer of the marks of the Godhead who wrapped a towel around his waist, took a basin of water and knelt to wash his followers' feet.

What would it mean in my setting—in the life of work, home or church—for me to 'wash another's feet'? And in what ways could the Church be seen to follow its Master's example?

2

BEING TRULY CLEAN

He came to Simon Peter, who said to him, 'Lord, are you going to wash my feet?' Jesus answered, 'You do not know now what I am doing, but later you will understand.' Peter said to him, 'You will never wash my feet.' Jesus answered, 'Unless I wash you, you have no share with me.' Simon Peter said to him, 'Lord, not my feet only but also my hands and my head!' Jesus said to him, 'One who has bathed does not need to wash, except for the feet, but is entirely clean. And you are clean, though not all of you.' For he knew who was to betray him; for this reason he said, 'Not all of you are clean.'

JOHN 13:6–11

Once again we are confronted with the mystery of 'knowing' and 'not knowing'. Peter 'did not know' what Jesus was doing by washing their feet (though he would, he was promised, 'later'). In contrast, Jesus 'knew' who was going to betray him—the one into whose heart the devil had already put the idea (13:2). In fact, all through this little scene Peter acts with an ignorance that borders on clumsiness, or possibly desperation. He *wants* to know, to be the one who is privy to the great plan, but, as at Caesarea Philippi, he always seems to get the wrong end of the stick (see Mark 8:29, 32–33).

Peter's refusal to let Jesus wash his feet might have been born of a variety of emotions. He may have been ashamed that he had sat by while his teacher took up the bowl and began the task. He may have felt that it was necessary to redress the balance in some way, to show at least a token humility. He may have felt that one of the more junior members of the group should be doing the task and was indicating that someone else, but not Jesus, should be washing his, Peter's, feet.

Whatever the reason, he had got it wrong. Jesus had not taken up the bowl to shame them, we are told, but to show the extent of his love. To reject a loving gesture is to reject the love itself. We all know how deeply wounding it is when an action offered out of love is curtly or brutally rejected. Jesus was not then, and has never been, in the 'blame' business. It was true that the disciples had behaved thoughtlessly. Perhaps one of them should have leapt up to seize a basin and perform this servant task. But Jesus was about a deeper purpose than trying to make them squirm.

Peter was never one to put things in ambiguous words. 'You will never wash my feet!' he asserts. Never! Such a fine, bold word, as total and ultimate as the love Jesus was showing them in this simple gesture of service. It is very dangerous to say 'never' to God about anything to do with human character, temperament or intention, because in every sense we are provisional beings. We are caught all the while by the very mortality in which God has clothed us. We aspire to be 'like gods' (as the serpent promised Eve) but always trip over the frailty of our humanity.

It happened again here. When Peter refused to be washed, Jesus gave him a gentle but profound warning: 'Unless I wash you, you have no share with me.' Sharing with Jesus, being part of his new people, was not something Peter could earn or demand. Only those who had received forgiveness from him, who had been (in the language of this Gospel) 'born anew' (3:3), could enjoy that privilege. Peter would not attain it by standing on his hurt dignity, but by submitting to the Master's gentle washing. It is a beautiful picture, and Peter—typically—responded with enthusiasm: 'Not my feet only but also my hands and my head!'

It's hard to work out what he meant. Was he conscious that his sins were as much the fruit of his mind and his hands as his erring feet? Or was it, more simply, that he just wanted to indicate that if being 'part' of Jesus was at stake, he would have everything that was going?

In fact, the offer was restricted to the feet, because, as Jesus pointed out, that was the meaning of the sign. The water in the bowl would wash from their feet the dust and sweat of that day's journey. That was its purpose. There were baths for the washing of the whole body, but they didn't take place several times a day. 'You [the word is plural] are clean': a little later Jesus will assure them that they *are* clean 'by the word that I have spoken to you' (15:3). But that cleansing of heart and mind which is at the heart of being 'born anew' does not rule out the possibility of our picking up dust and dirt from the day's journey. Few of us would wish to claim that we could go through a whole day without something occurring for which we feel we need divine forgiveness—but we don't need to be born again multiple times to achieve it!

This is a helpful picture of an experience that is fundamental to the Christian life. Those who are 'in Christ', by belief and baptism, are forgiven people; yet day by day they also need to seek cleansing from the bits of rubbish that have stuck to them in the course of each day's journey, through their own 'negligence, weakness or deliberate fault'. It explains why many Christians follow the discipline of an act of repentance and confession at the end of each day, and enjoy the assurance of forgiveness that goes with it. John returns to the same theme in his first letter: 'If we say that we have no sin, we deceive ourselves, and the truth is not in us. If we confess our sins, God who is faithful and just will forgive us our sins and cleanse us from all unrighteousness' (1 John 1:8–9).

Of course, there was one person present, as Jesus said, who was *not* clean—the one whose heart had been open to the devil's prompting. Presumably Judas had his feet washed, like the rest. But his heart was fatally soiled, and for that, it seemed, no remedy would be found.

An occasional churchgoer once remarked to me that Christians seemed to go to church each week and confess the same sins over and over again. 'Don't you get any better?' she asked. How would you have answered her?

3

THE TRUE SERVANT

After he had washed their feet, had put on his robe, and had returned to the table, he said to them, 'Do you know what I have done to you? You call me Teacher and Lord—and you are right, for that is what I am. So if I, your Lord and Teacher, have washed your feet, you also ought to wash one another's feet. For I have set you an example, that you also should do as I have done to you. Very truly, I tell you, servants are not greater than their master, nor are messengers greater than the one who sent them. If you know these things, you are blessed if you do them.'

JOHN 13:12–17

'Do you *know* what I have done to you?' There it is again—the question of 'knowledge'. They 'knew' that he had washed their feet, but its deeper meaning, the significance of this dramatic gesture, was still beyond their comprehension. But not for long, because Jesus was about to explain, in terms that are absolutely clear and precise.

They called him 'Teacher' and 'Lord'. And quite right, too—that was exactly what he was to them. But he, their Lord and Teacher, had just washed their feet. From this action, they were to learn (which is what you do from a teacher), and the lesson they were to learn was twofold.

First, in practical terms, following his example, they should 'wash one another's feet'. As his disciples they should learn not to stand on their dignity or demand rights, but to take the path of humble service. That was the way that Jesus had trodden and it was the way he expected of his followers.

Second, they should learn an important principle. It is introduced by a typical 'formula', often translated in the older Bibles as 'Verily, verily' or in more modern ones by 'In truth I tell you', 'Truly, I tell you', or here 'Very truly, I tell you'. The original is a simple repetition of the word 'amen', which means 'so be it', 'truth' or 'certainly'. What Jesus actually said was, '*Amen, amen*', as though what followed was to be underlined or put into italics. These 'amen' sayings of Jesus are often a kind of summary of an argument already made at greater length, or the application of a principle from an event or argument. Perhaps they should be underlined in red, or something like that, in our Bibles.

This 'amen, amen' saying concerns the relationship of the sender to the ones who are sent, and of servants to their master. It is the greater one who sends, or who commands the servants. The messengers (the word is 'apostles', literally) do not bear their own message but the message of the one who sent them. The servants don't perform their own will but the will of their master or mistress. In one sense it's commonplace and obvious. But here Jesus applied it both to himself ('I have come... not to do my own will, but the will of *him who sent me*', John 6:38) and to the disciples whom he was to 'send out' with his message. He and they were servants and messengers—Jesus of his Father, the disciples of their 'Lord and Teacher'. It was a lesson finally and memorably expressed in the same room on the day of his resurrection, when he breathed on the disciples and said, 'As the Father sent me, I am sending you' (20:21).

'Teacher' and 'Lord' express two different aspects of the relationship of Jesus to his disciples. 'Disciples' are those who follow a teacher, who sit at his feet and drink in his wisdom. Literally, they are 'learners'. Many people today have no problem with the idea of Jesus as a great teacher, even perhaps the greatest religious teacher the world has seen. But it is a step further to call that teacher 'Lord'. Some of those, at least, who are prepared to speak well of Jesus as teacher hold back from accepting him as Lord in the sense that he should have a controlling influence on their lives. That, after all, is its meaning here—the 'Lord' was the one who gave orders to his servants, and the servants acknowledged his 'lordship'.

Christian faith has always, and necessarily, demanded more of believers than that they should simply recognize the depth and truth of the teachings of Jesus. As he himself constantly affirmed, this was not truth to be debated or assented to, but truth to be *done*. Even saying 'Lord, Lord!' was not enough, unless the one who proclaimed his lordship did 'the will of the Father in heaven' (see Matthew 7:21). To call Jesus 'Lord' is to recognize his authority, not just in some theoretical way but in a life of daily obedience. One logical consequence of this is that we can't 'pick and mix' with his teaching, choosing the bits we like but rejecting what we find uncongenial or unacceptable.

The Gospels tell us over and over again that Jesus spoke 'with authority', unlike the scribes and teachers of the law (see, for example, Matthew 7:29 and 9:8). The difference was that Jesus spoke on his own authority whereas the scribes simply passed on their own interpretation or application of laws that already existed. People might legitimately question their interpretation—and many did. But Jesus spoke in a way that brooked no contradiction. His teaching was not material for debate but for action. It is a crucial difference—the difference between a primary authority and a secondary one; or, to put it more bluntly, an invitation to consider and a call to obedience. Jesus was, and is, Teacher *and Lord*. That is what gives his words real authority. This is truth to be acted upon.

But that, as Jesus reminded his disciples, is not the same as imposing a legalistic burden on them, weighing them down with rules and regulations. Like the psalmist of old, he saw God's will as conveying delight, joy and freedom when fully accepted. 'I find my delight in your commandments', sings

Psalm 119:47. Similarly, the teaching of Jesus is not going to be a burden but a blessing to his followers: 'If you know these things, you are blessed if you do them.'

How could we convince a culture which hates rules, regulations and restrictions that following the teaching of Jesus is a liberating process, a path to blessing? And what, in practical terms, does it mean to accept Jesus not only as Teacher but as Lord?

4

THE COMING OF THE NIGHT

'I am not speaking of all of you; I know whom I have chosen. But it is to fulfil the scripture, "The one who ate my bread has lifted his heel against me." I tell you this now, before it occurs, so that when it does occur, you may believe that I am he. Very truly, I tell you, whoever receives one whom I send receives me; and whoever receives me receives him who sent me.' After saying this Jesus was troubled in spirit, and declared, 'Very truly, I tell you, one of you will betray me.' The disciples looked at one another, uncertain of whom he was speaking. One of his disciples—the one whom Jesus loved—was reclining next to him; Simon Peter therefore motioned to him to ask Jesus of whom he was speaking. So while reclining next to Jesus, he asked him, 'Lord, who is it?' Jesus answered, 'It is the one to whom I give this piece of bread when I have dipped it in the dish.' So when he had dipped the piece of bread, he gave it to Judas son of Simon Iscariot. After he received the piece of bread, Satan entered into him. Jesus said to him, 'Do quickly what you are going to do.' Now no one at the table knew why he said this to him. Some thought that, because Judas had the common purse, Jesus was telling him, 'Buy what we need for the festival'; or, that he should give something to the poor. So, after receiving the piece of bread, he immediately went out. And it was night.

JOHN 13:18–30

The preliminaries were now over. Feet had been washed and dried. The point had been made. It was time for the meal, and we can imagine that the slightly embarrassed disciples were glad to move to their places around the table and turn to happier things—or so they thought. But this was to be no ordinary evening meal, not even an ordinary Passover one.

Among those reclining around the low table, in the manner of the time, were two people picked out by the narrator. One is the disciple whom 'Jesus loved' and the other the disciple who betrayed him. They were, of course, actual and real people, one an unnamed person who was the source, if not the author, of this fourth Gospel, the other Judas Iscariot. But they can also stand for two contrasting responses to Jesus and, in that sense, are in themselves symbolic and typical.

Take first the 'disciple Jesus loved'. The question of his identity is at the heart of the mystery of this Gospel. Who is this strange figure who crops up crucially in the narrative from time to time and finally, in its closing sentences, reveals that he is its author, or at any rate its source of information (see 21:24)? Is he, as some have suggested, Lazarus, because he is the only man identified in the book as someone whom Jesus 'loved' (11:3)? But surely, the moment he is named, this careful anonymity must be destroyed. The oldest and, for me, most convincing identification is with John, the brother of James and son of Zebedee. He was certainly an 'eye-witness', and the meticulous way in which this Gospel manages to avoid actually naming him is a powerful piece of evidence (see, for example, 1:35–40). Whoever the beloved disciple was, his role is that of Christ's confidant, the one to whom things are revealed that are not to be known even by the rest of the disciples.

We may find the description 'the disciple Jesus loved' comforting or disturbing. It is, in a sense, comforting to know that Jesus not only had a loving heart for all who turned to him, but also needed and enjoyed the intimacy of 'particular' people—Mary and Martha; Lazarus; his mother; and this anonymous 'beloved disciple'. It tells us that the love of others which Jesus required of his followers is not distorted or invalidated by their love for particular people—a close friend, a marriage partner, children or grandchildren. Christ's love for particular 'special' people did not affect, and was never accused of affecting, the love he showed for all his friends and those people who came to him with various needs.

The disturbing element lies in the notion that Jesus, the Son of God, had 'favourites'—but that can be rejected out of hand. To love one person in a special way is not at all the same as 'favouritism', which is an ugly and subtle form of discrimination. The Gospel records offer not a hint of an idea that Jesus gave preferential treatment to people he 'liked'—otherwise, why did he tell the rich young man, who evoked his 'love', that he would be excluded from eternal life if he clung to his wealth (Mark 10:21–22)? God has no favourites—a truth Peter learnt painfully (Acts 10:34)—and neither does his Son. But that did not prevent him, as a facet of his real humanity, from valuing a particular confidant and friend. So may we, his followers, providing always that we follow the example of Jesus and do not allow our particular love to be corrupted into favouritism or partiality.

So, here, only 'John', reclining next to Jesus (literally 'in his bosom', close to his chest), was privy to the clue that the betrayer would prove to be the one to whom Jesus gave the morsel of bread dipped in the dish—a sign of special love and favour, it must be said. The tragedy is that Judas *could* also have been a 'beloved disciple', but he chose another path. The 'beloved' disciple is the one who is 'in the bosom of Jesus', just as this Gospel has already told us that Jesus is 'in the bosom of the Father' (1:18)—a person enjoying an intimacy of relationship, a 'special' friend, one with whom secrets and intentions may be shared.

Yet the message of Jesus in this discourse, as we shall see, is that *all* of his disciples are his 'friends'—'if they do what I command'—and all will be privy to his 'secrets'. What the 'beloved disciple' was, we may all be in the new community that Jesus was calling to himself. In that community, there are no favourites, because all are, in a sense, his particular friends. All, as John tells the churches later in his life, may 'abide' in the love of God and all may know that the love of God abides in them (1 John 4:16). By grace we can all be 'disciples Jesus loves'.

The contrast with Judas is stark, as it is surely meant to be. It is almost impossible to fathom what was going on in his tortured mind. Just before these events, he had effectively been rebuked by Jesus over his attitude to Mary's costly gift of the perfume of pure nard with which she anointed the master's feet. This little incident may well have been the last straw for Judas—yet another piece of evidence that Jesus was an impractical dreamer rather than the dynamic Son of David for whom he had been looking (see 12:4–8). At any rate, it was directly after this that he made his approach to the chief priests with the offer to betray Jesus to the authorities (see Mark 14:10, and notice the word 'then').

Whatever Judas' human motivation, John is clear that his action was the consequence of giving way to the devil. It was 'the devil' who 'put it into the heart of Judas... to betray him' and now it was 'after receiving the piece of bread' offered by Jesus that 'Satan entered into him'. Here is the mystery of evil illustrated in all its complexity. A chosen disciple, one who had seen the miraculous signs, heard the wonderful teaching, and observed the openness of Jesus to human need, could nevertheless fail to resist the temptation.

But what *was* that temptation? Surely thirty pieces of silver would not have been enough to undermine his loyalty? Was it exasperation at the non-violent, open, patient approach of Jesus? Was it a mad desire to bring things to a head and spark a final confrontation between the power of God and the powers of evil? Was it envy of those who were closer to the master and seemed to enjoy his confidence? Whatever the reason, as Richard Burridge points out in his commentary on this passage, the reality of temptation does not absolve him of responsibility: 'there have been several appeals to him during this meal', including Jesus' offer to him of the special mark of respect signified by the gift of the dipped morsel, usually reserved for the most honoured guest.

But he rejected those appeals, his 'heart' now wide open to other and more sinister influences. It is a sobering thought to reflect that if this can happen to someone so close to Jesus, it is something that every disciple must constantly guard against. Just as we can all be the 'disciple Jesus loved', so it is sadly true that we may all be 'the disciple who betrayed him'.

And it was night. The words are as stark in Greek as they are in English. Perhaps, as Judas went out, the all-seeing observer noticed that darkness had fallen, and added this detail to his account. Light and darkness have been great themes of his book, from the 'light of all people' (1:4) and the 'light of the world' (9:5), represented by Jesus, to the darkness of rejection (3:19) and the 'hour of darkness' when people 'stumble' (9:4; 11:10). Now night has its moment. Darkness closes in on the little apostolic band and their master.

What was it that distinguished the 'disciple Jesus loved' from the one who betrayed him? Was it background, upbringing, temperament, ambition, faith (or its absence) or some spiritual weakness at the heart of the man? What steps could a disciple take to ensure that they remain in the love of Jesus, and shut their hearts and minds to destructive temptations?

THE PROMISED HELPER

5

THE NEW COMMANDMENT

When he had gone out, Jesus said, 'Now the Son of Man has been glorified, and God has been glorified in him. If God has been glorified in him, God will also glorify him in himself and will glorify him at once. Little children, I am with you only a little longer. You will look for me; and as I said to the Jews so now I say to you, "Where I am going, you cannot come." I give you a new commandment, that you love one another. Just as I have loved you, you also should love one another. By this everyone will know that you are my disciples, if you have love for one another.' Simon Peter said to him, 'Lord, where are you going?' Jesus answered, 'Where I am going, you cannot follow me now; but you will follow afterward.' Peter said to him, 'Lord, why can I not follow you now? I will lay down my life for you.' Jesus answered, 'Will you lay down your life for me? Very truly, I tell you, before the cock crows, you will have denied me three times.'

JOHN 13:31–38

The prologue to the discourse has almost ended. The disciples have been 'washed', their future role as Christ's messengers affirmed, and the betrayer has been identified. It would seem that the meal was now over and the extended 'after-dinner speech', the farewell discourse, can begin. Several important disclosures sum up the evening so far.

Firstly, Judas had 'gone out', in more senses than one—gone out, never to be part of the company of the apostles again. Of all the Gospel writers, John seems to have the least sympathy for Judas, possibly because he alone was aware of the giving of the morsel of bread, and of the way Judas spurned that last gesture of love from Jesus. The die was cast, and from now on the events that were destined would happen in swift succession.

Secondly, there was the first expression of the 'new commandment', that they should 'love one another' in the same way that Jesus had loved them. This commandment was not new in the sense that God's people had always been enjoined to show love to neighbour as well as to God, but it *was* new in its application and demands. Of course they should love their neighbours, a point that Jesus had emphasized many times in his teaching. But that is a general commandment for all people and at all times—witness the parable of the good Samaritan. But now they were enjoined to love *each other*, the fellow citizens of the kingdom of God, their co-members in the body of Christ, and to love them in a particular way—'as I have loved you'.

The love of Jesus is self-sacrificing love. That was what they would learn with dreadful clarity over the next few days. This was what it meant that 'God so loved the world that he gave his only Son' (3:16). This was what it meant that the Son of Man had come to 'give his life a ransom for many' (Mark 10:45). We shall shortly see how Jesus defined love in these very terms on this last evening with his friends.

What was at stake here was the unity and love of the tiny community which Jesus would leave behind, entrusting it with the daunting task of carrying on his mission in the world. Love is the only mortar that can hold people together through the kind of trials they would face. Love, indeed, became the badge and hallmark of the early Church. As the Roman writer Tertullian put it so memorably, 'See how these Christians love each other.'

A third disclosure, if we can call it that, was Peter's bravado and its consequent rebuke. Here is the supreme example of someone who, at least at this stage of his experience, simply could not learn from his mistakes. Faced with the prospect of Jesus going away, and being told that he couldn't follow him now but would do later (as he would 'later' understand about the full meaning of the foot-washing), Peter exploded in protest: 'Why can I not follow you now? I will lay down my life for you.'

The reply of Jesus must have come like a drenching bucket of cold water on the fire of his indignation. '*Die* for me? Before the night is over, you will have denied me three times.'

So at last the scene has been set. The hour has come. 'Now the Son of Man has been glorified.' We are forced to ask, 'How?' By being betrayed by one of his own disciples? By another one being told that his loyalty won't even last the night? By the falling of the darkness outside or the troubling of spirit on the inside?

This use of the word 'glorified' is another of the mysteries of the fourth Gospel, but clearly the writer is using it to refer to the great saving event that was now set in train. With the traitor scurrying off to the temple, there was now no going back. 'As it is written', the Son of Man 'will be delivered into the hands of evil men and crucified'. Jesus had told them that many times (see Luke 24:7). But he had also added the words which at this stage they seem to have overlooked: '…and on the third day rise again'. In that sequence of events, not only God would be 'glorified', as his great purpose of love for the human race was worked out, but so would be his Son. The one who is now apparently captive to events would be set gloriously free—free to 'bring many sons and daughters to glory' (Hebrews 2:10).

The Bible tells us to love our neighbours. Jesus went beyond that, calling his followers to love their enemies, and to love one another in a self-giving way. How can Christians today show those kinds of love in the society in which they live? And would a modern commentator invite his readers to 'see how these Christians love each other', as Tertullian did in the second century? Is there a message in that for the Church today?

6

A PLACE PREPARED

'Do not let your hearts be troubled. Believe in God, believe also in me. In my Father's house there are many dwelling places. If it were not so, would I have told you that I go to prepare a place for you? And if I go and prepare a place for you, I will come again and will take you to myself, so that where I am, there you may be also.'

JOHN 14:1–3

These words are very well known but seldom read in their context. That's partly the fault of the chapter divisions, which were not part of the original text. The previous chapter ended with the chilling warning of Jesus to his friends that he would soon be leaving them and that where he was going they could not come, followed by the equally daunting warning to Peter that he would deny his master three times before the rooster crowed the next morning. No wonder their hearts were 'troubled'.

Jesus had already spoken of his own heart being 'troubled', indeed, 'deeply troubled'—which is the implication of 'in spirit' (13:21)—so this meal together was at this moment proving less than the festive occasion they had expected. One can imagine the mood changing from friendly banter and laughter as the disciples slowly began to sense that this was indeed an evening of destiny, and that they were inescapably caught up in it. Jesus sensed their mood—'troubled', anxious, baffled. What did all this mean, this talk of 'going away' and leaving them, of betrayal and denial and laying down one's life?

That is the context for this marvellous exhortation in 14:1–3. As he looked around the table at his friends, we can imagine Jesus longing for them to know and understand God's purpose in it all, wishing that he could somehow set their troubled hearts at rest. What he could do was to call them again to simple trust. He didn't expect them to understand fully, and where we can't understand it is very hard to believe. What he did call them to do was to *trust*, not in a set of propositions about death and resurrection or eternal life but in two utterly reliable persons, the Father and the Son. 'Believe…' he said (it could equally well be translated, 'You believe…') 'in God, believe also in me.'

This takes us back a few days to the story of the raising of Lazarus. Jesus asked Martha whether she believed that he was 'the resurrection and the life'. She probably found that a proposition too far, but she was able to blurt out in utter sincerity, 'Yes, Lord, I believe that you are the Messiah, the Son of God' (John 11:25–27).

That is why these words spoken to the disciples in the upper room are appropriate for a funeral service, where they are often read. The call to the 'troubled hearts' of the mourners at that moment is not to embrace an array of doctrines about eternal life, but to turn in simple trust to the Father and the Son, to put our faith in this quietly spoken Lord and Teacher who speaks with such authority about these matters.

In his Father's house there is no shortage of accommodation: there are 'many dwelling places'. The word used (*monai*) literally means 'places to abide', usually on a journey. Our modern equivalent would be motels, I suppose—or, more literally, 'travel lodges'! They don't represent the final destination, but places to rest on the journey, and the concept of journeys runs strongly through these sayings. Jesus himself was going on a journey, he told them, one on which they couldn't join him at the present, but—what a rich promise!—one whose purpose was to 'prepare a place for you… so that where I am, there you may be also'. This 'place' is also a travel lodge, a stop on a journey that will continue to a destination he was shortly to reveal to them.

What Jesus said to comfort their troubled hearts has been a source of perpetual comfort and assurance to Christians down the ages. The journey of faith that we embark on here on earth does not end at death, but goes beyond into unimaginable regions of the spirit. We are travellers on a journey, as those first disciples were. In one sense that can be a disturbing, rather than comforting, thought. What lies ahead? What is there beyond that veil that separates earth from heaven, the material world from the spiritual one? Perhaps we fear a journey that may take us into misty realms of discarnate beings, a sort of dream world of the spirit.

But these words should dispel such anxieties. Wherever we go and whatever path we are called to follow, the believer travels not alone but in the company of Jesus. He is the 'dragoman', the attendant who goes ahead of the travellers to prepare the next night's stopping place, to light a fire, perhaps, and to prepare some food. At each stage of the journey into what we may call the 'unknown', we know well who will be there ahead of us, 'preparing the place', inviting us in ('take you to myself') and offering us his company ('so that where I am, there you may be also'). We are all travellers on the journey of life. Death is not its terminus but a staging-post, a point of change and transition. At that moment of transition nothing is so reassuring as to know the presence of a familiar figure, especially when it is of someone who has already gone that way and knows the route. That is the reassurance Jesus offered here to his disciples, and offers today to those who believe in him and in the Father.

So the disciples, and those who follow in their life of faith down through the ages, will never be abandoned. That is why they can 'set their troubled hearts at rest' (14:1, REB).

It is not difficult to think of this life as a journey. In the context of our own faith-journeys, can we begin to imagine what it might mean to resume that pilgrimage on the other side of the divide that we call death? What fears may we have about that eventuality?

7

WAY, TRUTH, LIFE

'And you know the way to the place where I am going.' Thomas
said to him, 'Lord, we do not know where you are going. How can
we know the way?' Jesus said to him, 'I am the way, and the truth,
and the life. No one comes to the Father except through me.'

JOHN 14:4–6

Not for the first time, nor the last, Thomas got the wrong end
of the stick. Jesus had spoken of a 'place' to which he was
going, and here asserted that they 'knew' the way to it. Sceptical
Thomas was baffled. They *didn't* know where he was going, let
alone the way to it Once again, so far as he was concerned,
Jesus was talking in riddles.

It's rather like his altercation with Jesus over the death of
Lazarus (John 11:11–16). Far from accepting that Jesus was
going to Lazarus 'to awaken him from sleep', as he had said,
Thomas could see only the despair of death: 'Let's go and die
with him.' Later, in this same room after the resurrection, it is
of course Thomas who finds it impossible to accept without
material proof the claim of the other disciples to have seen Jesus
alive. In the apostolic band, he was the statutory sceptic, but no
less a disciple for all that.

Here Jesus addresses to him words that have entered into the
heart of Christian belief and mission. The way *to* God, the truth
about God and the life *of* God are all to be found in his Son. It
is a kind of summary of everything that the Gospel has so far

revealed to us about Jesus and his purpose in the world. The other sayings that begin 'I am…' seem to lead up to this one. Jesus is the door, the light of the world, the good shepherd, the bread of life and the resurrection of the dead. He is all these things because in him 'the Father' has been pleased to reveal himself with unique clarity.

To that 'place' of eternal life he is the way. That is much more than saying that he 'shows us the way', though he does. He is both the signpost and the path. A friend once told me of asking an Arab in Jerusalem the way to the Damascus Gate. The man offered him no instructions, but simply took his arm and said, 'I am the way'—and led him there. It is in exactly that sense that Jesus is the way to God. He leads us there. Not without reason, the first Christians were called 'followers of the Way'—and that 'way' was Christ.

Jesus is also 'the truth'. That says more than that he *tells* the truth (though he does). He *is* the truth: he exemplifies it, represents it, reveals it in himself. I suppose this is a vivid way of saying what Christians have always believed—that in Jesus God revealed himself more fully and completely than he has ever done in any other way. It doesn't mean that there is no truth without him, because that would, for example, devalue all the profound truths about God that were revealed to people before Christ. It could hardly be argued that Abraham, Moses, David and the great Hebrew prophets knew nothing of God! But there is a completeness and transparency about the revelation of God in Jesus that we believe to be unique.

And Jesus is 'the life'. 'In him was life,' said John in the prologue to this Gospel (1:4)—which again is saying more than that he was 'alive'. In some way Jesus shared the source of life itself: 'that life was the light of humankind'. He has the gift of life and he has the authority to give life to 'whom he is pleased to give it' (see John 5:21). Again, this is more than ordinary, breathing, mortal life. 'I have come that they may have life, and have it to the full' (John 10:10). Indeed, had he not just told

Martha, 'I am the resurrection *and the life*'? All of these ideas are implicit in the apparently simple words, 'I am the life'.

'I am the way, and the truth, and the life.' That is a huge claim, a claim that speaks of divine authority and power. But it seems to be exceeded by the statement that followed: 'No one comes to the Father except through me.'

These words can be, and have been, used by Christians as a stick with which to beat people of other faiths. 'Only one way,' we say, 'and that way is Jesus.' The implication is that all other paths to 'the Father' ultimately lead nowhere, and that no one can approach God except through his Son Jesus. But that, at its simplest, would make nonsense of the statement in Acts 10:4 that the prayers of Cornelius, a God-fearing but non-Christian Roman, had 'come up as a memorial offering before God'. He was not, at that point, coming to the Father through Jesus, because he knew little or nothing about him. Equally, of course—taken literally—it would mean that all those great saints, prophets and patriarchs of the Old Testament were wasting their time in prayer and worship, seeing that they were not coming to the Father through the Son.

So the words of Jesus must mean rather more than meets the eye—which is only to say that they are like many other sayings in this Gospel. Clearly this does represent a staggering claim, and there is no point in denying it. Jesus, as the Son of God, could alone provide reliable revelation of the Father and open the way for people to come to him for forgiveness and salvation. In that sense, there really *is* 'no other way'. I like the way Richard Burridge, a distinguished New Testament scholar, explains the significance of this saying in his *People's Bible Commentary* on John: 'Only one who has come from God, from the infinite, can become the bridge whereby finite human beings come to God. Whenever anyone, of whatever belief, finds truth and life in God they come through the way of Jesus, whether they realize it or not.'

What would it mean to share with people of other faiths and cultures this particular truth of the Christian faith while also recognizing the many different paths by which people approach their Creator?

8

SEEING THE FATHER

'If you know me, you will know my Father also. From now on you do know him and have seen him.' Philip said to him, 'Lord, show us the Father, and we will be satisfied.' Jesus said to him, 'Have I been with you all this time, Philip, and you still do not know me? Whoever has seen me has seen the Father. How can you say, "Show us the Father"? Do you not believe that I am in the Father and the Father is in me? The words that I say to you I do not speak on my own; but the Father who dwells in me does his works. Believe me that I am in the Father and the Father is in me; but if you do not, then believe me because of the works themselves.'

JOHN 14:7–11

Thomas asked his question, typical of his sceptical approach to things. Now the down-to-earth Philip asks his. The last time John recorded some words of his, they had a similarly earthy quality—Philip seems to have had little time for what he would probably have called 'airy-fairy' notions. Faced with a huge and hungry crowd, and Jesus' question as to how they might feed them all, Philip did a bit of simple mathematics and worked out that two hundred denarii (say, over £3000) wouldn't be enough to buy bread for all of them. It wasn't that Philip didn't believe in Jesus, with all his heart. He had been a faithful disciple, and brought his friend Nathanael to the Lord as well (John 1:45–46). But he was not at home in the world of spirituality. In other words, he was like quite a few of us.

Here, faced with the statement that 'from now on you do know (the Father) and have seen him' he blurted out, 'Show us the Father, and we will be satisfied.' *Show* us! All of these mysterious words and ideas were flying around, but Philip wanted to earth it all in terms he could grasp. He knew Jesus, certainly. But there remained a goal beyond that. Jesus spoke constantly about 'the Father': would it be so difficult to give them just a glimpse of him?

Philip is not the first devout person to long for a vision of God, the final answer to doubt, the ultimate assurance of faith. If only we could see! It was the request of Moses at the end of his life. The psalmist frequently pleads to see God's glory. Yet, as the prologue of this Gospel reminds us, 'No one has ever seen God' (1:18a). For all their longing and their prayers, the 'beatific vision' is reserved for heaven.

Yet—and this was what Jesus had already hinted at—the disciples had a unique opportunity to 'see God' in Jesus. Again, the Prologue points to this: 'It is God the only Son, who is close to the Father's heart, who has made him known' (1:18b). But now it is spelt out. 'Have I been with you all this time, Philip, and you still do not know me? Whoever has seen me has seen the Father. How can you say, "Show us the Father"? Do you not believe that I am in the Father and the Father is in me?'

The first 'you' is plural, addressed to them all. Jesus had been among them (all) for more than two years. Yet 'you' (singular, Philip) can still ask to see the Father. Haven't you learnt anything? Haven't you seen God himself at work? Haven't you seen the lame walk, the lepers cleansed, the blind receive their sight and even the dead restored to life? Haven't you heard my words, experienced my love, become my friends? How much more evidence do you need that the Father dwells in me, and I dwell in the Father?

This is the great unfolding mystery in John's Gospel, that God himself 'made his dwelling'—'abided'—in Jesus. Slowly the picture has unfolded of one who speaks with the voice of

God, reveals the love of God, does the works of God. By now, Jesus implied, the message should have sunk home. But even if they (it's back to plural now) cannot believe on the authority of the words of Jesus, surely they are convinced by the 'works'— the 'signs' that he has offered them, each in itself evidence of God at work on earth.

This was a crucial moment in the disciples' journey of discovery. On the eve of the crucifixion, they were being faced with an enormous, almost unthinkable truth, barely within human comprehension and shocking to the point of blasphemy to devout Jews. Here before them was a man (there was no doubt of that, a *man*, not an angel) who claimed to speak the words of God and do his works. Not only that, but everything they knew of him made the claim credible. Could it really be that their friend and teacher, with whom they had shared nights under the stars, caught fish and walked the dusty lanes of Galilee, was in truth at one with the creator of the universe? Could it be that Yahweh himself, the God of Abraham, Isaac and Jacob, 'dwelt' in this 33-year-old human being who shared the table with them that night?

Put it like that, and you begin to see what an amazing step of faith it was that brought the disciples to the unwavering belief that it was so. He was inviting them to look at him, as he reclined at the table, and 'see the Father'. Any human being who offered such an invitation was either stark, staring mad, totally deluded, or utterly confident of his relationship with God. They looked at Jesus, and made up their minds. It is the testimony of scripture that they believed him. It is the evidence of history that it cost all but one of them his life.

If to 'see Jesus' is to 'see God', what can we deduce about the nature and character of God from doing so? And how, in practice, does a Christian two thousand years after the incarnation 'see' Jesus?

9

ASKING IN MY NAME

'Very truly, I tell you, the one who believes in me will also do the works that I do and, in fact, will do greater works than these, because I am going to the Father. I will do whatever you ask in my name, so that the Father may be glorified in the Son. If in my name you ask me for anything, I will do it.'

JOHN 14:12–14

Here is another of the 'Amen, amen' sayings, underlining its significance for his hearers. 'Remember this after I am gone,' Jesus said in effect. 'This is important.' He then told them that after his departure they would 'do the works' that he did; his 'work' would be continued by them, and indeed multiplied. This is in one sense the expected theme of a 'farewell discourse' —what the founder has begun, his followers are to continue and develop. But the promise of Jesus is more specific than that: this would happen '*because*' he was going to the Father, not *despite* the fact.

That is the context of the promise that his followers would do 'greater works' than he had done. This wasn't—as some people have interpreted it—a challenge to them to outperform his own miracles and signs, but a promise that his departure would release a new power and authority among them. The precise identity of this new power had yet to be revealed to them, but Jesus was whetting their appetites, as it were, for the revelation he was shortly to make.

To be told that they would do 'greater works' than he had done must have staggered the disciples. They had seen what the 'works' of Jesus had been. They had stood by while the blind received sight, the lame walked, the lepers ran off cleansed and even the dead were raised to life. It had all been mind-blowing in its intensity, to the extent that they were probably still trying to come to terms with it. Had they really seen these things with their own eyes? Had the lanes and shores of Galilee *really* seen such miracles? As Jesus had said to them, 'Many prophets and righteous people longed to see what you see, but did not see it, and to hear what you hear, but did not hear it' (Matthew 13:17). This handful of men—and women?—who sat around him were uniquely privileged, there could be no denying that. But now to be told that what they had seen would be exceeded, not by another or greater Messiah but by themselves, must have beggared imagination.

In fact, the promise was much wider than that. These 'greater works' would be performed by 'the one who believes in me'. Jesus could look ahead, as he does later in this discourse, to other people in the future who would also believe in him 'through their word' (17:20). This promise would apply to them, too, which brings present-day believers in Jesus within its scope. We, too, may expect to share in these 'greater works'.

This promise has led some Christians to assume that Jesus expected the future Church to perform greater miracles than he had done, which seems a fantastic notion. In fact, the promise is not about the *nature* of the 'works', but their *extent*. Because Jesus was going to the Father—and that phrase is the clue to the whole passage—the power that had been present in him would in future be available much more widely.

That, at least, has been fulfilled. During the incarnation the ministry of Jesus and his miraculous works were necessarily limited, both in time and space, to something less than three years and one small territory at the eastern end of the Mediterranean. But when he had 'gone to the Father', that same power and authority would be available without such limitations, through those who would come to believe in him wherever they were.

We can see this happening in the early years of the Church, as described in the Acts of the Apostles: miracles were done in the name of Jesus in many places throughout Asia Minor and eastern Europe. Later, at many times in the Church's history, similar miracles have been reported, often associated with periods of great spiritual renewal and blessing. It would take a bold person to assert that 'miracles never happen today', though they occur hardly with the regularity that marked the ministry of Jesus. That, however, would not invalidate the terms of this promise, for now the healing and saving touch of Christ is made available to millions upon millions of people in literally every corner of the earth.

The final verses of this chapter make what may seem to be an even more amazing promise, that 'whatever [and anything] you ask in my name' will be done. We can't take the words 'anything' and 'whatever' in an entirely literal sense, however, because they are twice qualified. It is 'whatever you ask *in my name*' and 'If *in my name* you ask me for anything' that make the promise conditional rather than absolute. This is no open cheque for personal whims or selfish desires to be met, nor even authority to demand that apparently reasonable requests (for healing, perhaps, or for success in an important examination) should be granted by God.

So what does it mean to ask 'in my name'? That seems to be the crux of the argument. Happily, Jesus himself provided the answer: 'so that the Father may be glorified in the Son'. This is not simply a question of whether or not a particular answered prayer would bring God praise and glory—we could argue that *all* answered prayers do that. It revolves around our understanding of 'glorification', which certainly in John's Gospel has a particular connotation. On almost every occasion when Jesus speaks of being 'glorified' by his Father, it is connected with his death and resurrection: 'The hour has come for the Son of man to be glorified' (12:23). This is not the glory of 'success' but of sacrifice, of humble submission to the Father's will.

The nearest this Gospel comes to a 'Gethsemane' is the desperate prayer that Jesus—his soul 'troubled'—contemplated uttering: 'Father, save me from this hour.' But he corrected himself: 'No, it is for this reason that I have come to this hour. Father, glorify your name.' At that point a voice from heaven said, 'I have glorified it, and I will glorify it again' (12:27, 28). There is the heart of 'glory', doing the will of the Father, and we shall pray fruitfully only when our prayers are in line with his will. It is certainly fruitless to pray *against* it.

But when we are at one with Father and the Son, in the unity of fellowship which Jesus already enjoyed (v. 11) and which, as he will soon unfold, his followers can also enjoy, then praying is the natural way of sharing in the will of God. That is asking 'in my name'—in accordance with his will and purpose. And it is that prayer which will always and gloriously be granted. That is how we can share in the 'greater works'.

Praying, in other words, is not a matter of persuading God to do what I want, however much it may seem right and good. Prayer is bringing my will into line with the will of God and sharing in his purposes.

There are two great promises here to the disciples of Jesus. One is that he will continue his gracious work of love through them, and extend it far and wide throughout the world. The second is that nothing can withstand prayer when it is truly prayed 'in his name'. In our own lives, and in the life of the Church, what is the significance of these promises?

10

Not as Orphans

'If you love me, you will keep my commandments. And I will ask the Father, and he will give you another Advocate, to be with you forever. This is the Spirit of truth, whom the world cannot receive, because it neither sees him nor knows him. You know him, because he abides with you, and he will be in you. I will not leave you orphaned; I am coming to you.'

JOHN 14:15–18

At last Jesus revealed to the disciples the source of the new power and authority that they were to receive after he left them. It would come from an 'Advocate', 'the Spirit of truth', who would be with them, unlike Jesus, 'forever'—literally, 'until the end of the age'. Much of the rest of the discourse is then given over to explaining to them this new element in their lives, this fresh 'presence'. The gift, Jesus said, would be for all those, presumably now and into the future, who 'love me' and 'keep my commandments'.

The title 'Advocate' is an intriguing one which has caused translators many headaches over the centuries. The King James Version's 'Comforter' has an appealing sound to it but—at any rate, in modern English—conveys too soft and cosy an image. Of course, the word originally meant 'one who gives strength', from the Latin *fortis*, and that is near the meaning of the Greek word *parakletos* used here in the Gospel.

However, it does not do justice to the dynamic meaning of

the word. *Parakletos* is literally 'one who is called along to assist', 'one who stands by another to plead their cause'. In modern English we are familiar with the title 'paramedic', someone who works alongside or near the doctors. The 'para' part of the word *parakletos* means 'with' or 'alongside' and the 'kletos' part means 'called' or 'invited'. So a 'paraclete' (the English spelling) is one called alongside to assist.

All of this is rather more than dry grammar, for here is the heart of a word of tremendous meaning and importance to the Christian. Jesus has promised us a *parakletos*, someone sent by the Father and the Son to be 'alongside' us as our divine Helper. As the picture of this Helper emerges, we, like the disciples in the upper room, can begin to sense what a unique and precious gift he is. It is interesting that Jesus told them that he would not only be 'with' (alongside) them but *in* them. He would, as we shall learn later, be an indwelling Spirit rather than a helpful stranger.

Jesus said that they already 'knew' this Helper, whereas the world was entirely ignorant of him. The disciples 'knew' the work of the Spirit, had been its witnesses, had themselves been drawn to Jesus by the power of the same Spirit, even though at this stage they couldn't have identified him. That is a reminder that every movement towards God and Christ is the work of the Spirit. 'No one can come to me unless the Father draws him... The Spirit gives life' (6:44, 63). All that had so far happened in their own journey of faith was the work of the Spirit, but now they were to be 'introduced' to him.

Conversely, 'the world' does not know him. This is to become a theme of the discourse—the antithesis between 'the world' and 'the Spirit'. The world here is the 'cosmos', which would normally be a neutral word describing the created order, the universe. But in John's writings it has a special and negative meaning—it is the world, no doubt, but the world organized *as though God did not exist*. So the Christians in his churches are urged not to 'love the world, or the things in the world', which are described as 'the desire of the flesh, the desire of the eyes, the pride in riches' (1 John 2:15, 16). This is contrasted with the life of those who 'do the will of God', who 'live for ever'.

In my early days as a committed Christian, 'worldly' was a word much bandied about. Going to the cinema was 'worldly'. Football matches were 'worldly'. Smoking, drinking and dancing were 'worldly'. Funnily enough, I don't recall any little booklets explaining that greed and self-indulgence, struggling for position, pride and envy, prejudice and indifference to injustice were also 'worldly', though they undoubtedly are. Anything that speaks of a lifestyle that ignores God's standards and holiness is 'worldly'. Conversely, to live in conformity with the will of God is to be a child of God's kingdom.

And that is to be the lifestyle of the disciples of Jesus from now on—loving him and 'keeping his commandments', so that they will receive the promised Advocate, who will stand by them and plead their cause.

Then they won't be 'orphans'—a very vivid way of putting it! The word used could refer to a child left without parents or to a follower left without a leader. In a sense, both describe the situation of the disciples. They had come to depend on Jesus in the way a child depends on his or her parents, and as rather stumbling followers it must have been hard for them to imagine life without the dynamic figure of Jesus to urge, encourage and lead them on the way. Without him, they would no doubt have felt like orphans.

Yet Jesus said, 'I will not leave you orphaned; I am coming to you.' Not surprisingly, as we shall see, the disciples found this rather baffling. Hadn't he told them that he was 'going away'— 'going to the Father'? So how could he say that he would be 'coming' to them? It would be explained to them quite soon in words, but their true assurance would not come until later, when the promise became their own experience of the Spirit.

The Victorian hymn writer William Chatterton Dix caught something of this challenge to faith rather well:

Alleluia, not as orphans
are we left in sorrow now;
Alleluia, he is near us,
faith believes, nor questions how...

The notion of the Holy Spirit as a Helper alongside us, and as an Advocate pleading our cause, may seem remote from everyday experience. In what circumstances might the Christian today feel the need for such a helper, or for a divine wisdom to argue our cause?

11

THE DIVINE RESIDENCE

'In a little while the world will no longer see me, but you will see me; because I live, you also will live. On that day you will know that I am in my Father, and you in me, and I in you. They who have my commandments and keep them are those who love me; and those who love me will be loved by my Father, and I will love them and reveal myself to them.' Judas (not Iscariot) said to him, 'Lord, how is it that you will reveal yourself to us, and not to the world?' Jesus answered him, 'Those who love me will keep my word, and my Father will love them, and we will come to them and make our home with them. Whoever does not love me does not keep my words; and the word that you hear is not mine, but is from the Father who sent me.'

JOHN 14:19–24

This extended seminar on the coming of the Spirit and the way in which the disciples will experience it now moves into even deeper territory. If Jesus is both 'going away' and at the same time 'coming to them', he owes them something of an explanation. At the moment, Jesus realizes that they will struggle to grasp the enormity of what he is saying to them. It is something that they will only truly comprehend in the future—'on that day'.

But here is its heart, set out in words of extreme simplicity. They could look forward to a time when Jesus would be 'in' his Father, the disciples would be 'in' him, and he would be 'in' them. The words were indeed simple, but the concept is profound. He had already linked their love of him with the keeping of his 'commandments'—observing what he has taught them. Soon he would tell them what the chief of those 'commandments' is. Now he explains that those who show their love for him in this way will be loved not only by Jesus, but also by the Father, and to these people Jesus will 'reveal himself'.

On each occasion that Jesus had talked about 'going away' one or other of the disciples had raised a question—Peter, Thomas and then Philip. Now it is the turn of a hitherto almost anonymous member of the Twelve, Judas (carefully identified as 'not Iscariot'). Luke 6:16 tells us that he was the son of James.

His question, like the saying of Jesus they had just heard, was deceptively simple. How was it that Jesus would reveal himself to them, but not to 'the world'? Actually the English preposition translates a phrase which could also mean 'why', but 'how' seems to make better sense in the context. How would this revelation of Jesus, this identifying of himself, be visible to some people and not to others?

Again Jesus restated the case. The whole thing revolved around love—love shown by 'keeping his word'. Those who do so will enjoy the Father's love and—a new idea—*we*, the Father and the Son, will 'come to them and make our home with them'. This picks up the idea of 'dwelling', which Jesus had raised earlier in connection with the 'Father's house' and its 'many dwelling places' which he was going to prepare for them. One day they would dwell with the Father, but one day *the Father would dwell with them*. Indeed, the promise is even more dramatic than that: the Father-Son partnership would 'make [their] home with them'. There is a wonderful sense of permanence in these words. Unlike their relationship on earth, soon to be brought to an abrupt end, this relationship would not be temporary. The word used for 'dwelling' is *mone*, in the singular 'home', the place where we 'abide' and are secure. As Richard

Burridge puts it, 'Not only does Jesus prepare a place for us in God, but he also makes a place for God in us.'

So much for those to whom Jesus would reveal himself. As for the others, what this Gospel calls 'the world', they are excluded from the promise not by the will of Jesus or the Father, but by their own rejection of the truth. Having no love for Jesus, they do not 'keep his words'. And the seriousness of that lies in the fact that the words he speaks and the disciples hear are not his, but the words of the one who sent him, the Father.

People often ask about heaven: what will it be like, who will be there, where is it to be found, how could it possibly contain all those for whom it is intended? The Bible answers those questions in two ways—with pictures ('The kingdom of heaven is *like*...'), or with the language of *relationships*. Here it is the latter. Our future dwelling will be in a 'place', but that place will not be found on a map or a chart of outer space. It is where God is, because the destiny of those who 'love Jesus and keep his word' is to dwell in God, and to be the dwelling place of God. If that sounds elusive, mystical or incomprehensible, it is at least definitive. Of course the whole notion of 'heaven' is beyond our ken, just as the notion of ordinary human life must be beyond the ken of the foetus in the womb. But just as that earthly life is the baby's destiny, so this heavenly life is ours. As the Anglican communion prayer puts it, '...that we may evermore dwell in him, and he in us'.

All of the pronouns in this passage are plural—'you', 'them', 'us'. That suggests that the first experience we will have of this 'heavenly' relationship with the Father-Son will be in the context of the Christian community, rather than in individual ecstasy. Is this how we experience the Church? Is your church, is mine, 'heavenly'?

TRUE PEACE

TEACHING AND REMINDING

'I have said these things to you while I am still with you. But the Advocate, the Holy Spirit, whom the Father will send in my name, will teach you everything, and remind you of all that I have said to you. Peace I leave with you; my peace I give to you. I do not give to you as the world gives. Do not let your hearts be troubled, and do not let them be afraid.'

JOHN 14:25–27

Once again Jesus put what he was saying to his friends into a time perspective. There are three tenses in the first sentence: 'I have said' is past tense, 'I am still with you' is present tense, and 'will send' and 'will teach' are future tense. He invited them to remember; he told them what his present intention was; and he made a firm promise about the future.

It seems that Jesus was only too aware that what he was telling them at that moment was beyond their comprehension. Certainly they were suffering from 'information overload'! In addition, they were in a highly tense and emotional frame of mind, only too conscious of his words about leaving them, and probably fearful of the future without his strong presence and wisdom. He was still with them, but everything he was saying had the ominous ring of inevitable change about it.

Human beings don't like change. At heart we are mostly conservative, happy with the familiar. The disciples were obviously not excessively cautious people—such would never 'drop their nets and follow' at the call of a passing prophet. But even they, caught up in the fraught atmosphere of first-century Jerusalem with its political intrigues and religious strife, could be excused for reflecting on the relative tranquillity that they had left behind in Galilee. Certainly the Gospels record their eagerness to get back there after the traumatic events which were to take place during the coming weekend.

They were 'troubled'—Jesus uses the same word again (see 14:1)—a word he had used to describe his own emotions in the face of what he knew lay ahead (12:27). He wanted to give them a parting gift of 'peace', but that gift would be but a part of a greater gift, the one he now called the 'Holy Spirit', the full and formal title of the third member of the Trinity, invoked under that name for the first time on the lips of Jesus in this Gospel. As devout Jews they were aware of this title, of course, employed by the psalmist—'Take not your Holy Spirit from me' (51:11)—and in Isaiah, where the Israelites of old are rebuked for having 'grieved God's Holy Spirit' (63:10). They knew him as the activity and presence of God himself. Now—a staggering thought—the self-same Holy Spirit was to be their personal teacher and mentor. He (or she—the word *pneuma* is feminine —and all that really matters is that we don't refer to the third person of the Trinity as 'it') was still, of course, the Advocate, the Helper who would stand alongside them in the future. But now they were to understand that he was nothing less than the Holy Spirit of God, sent by the Father, but in the name of Jesus—'in my name'.

The disciples may well have been reassured that this promised gift, awesome in title and nature, would come to them in the name of their beloved master. Probably of more importance was the promise that the Holy Spirit would 'teach' and 'remind' them of all that Jesus had said and was now saying to them.

This promise was regarded as of crucial importance in the early centuries of the Church, when there were many disputes over the teaching of Jesus and the meaning of his life, death and resurrection. It was because of these words of Jesus that special authority was given to those writings that the Church considered to be 'apostolic', because they were the work of, or authorized by, people who received this promise. That became the chief criterion for inclusion in what came to be the canon of New Testament scripture, as the Church slowly went through the often controversial process of sifting the many, many writings of the early years of Christianity.

Paul was added to the 'company of the apostles'—in his own words, 'as one untimely born' (1 Corinthians 15:8)—because he 'saw' Jesus on the road to Damascus. So far as other writings were concerned, it was the hallmark of apostolic authority for which the Church Fathers were looking. There may be (indeed, there are) disputes about whether they always got it right, but there was no disputing the reasoning behind the process. Jesus himself had promised a special gifting of the Holy Spirit to ensure that his teaching and indeed 'everything he had told them' would be passed on to his future followers.

That is why the early Church quickly came to give an authority to the apostolic writings that equalled, and in practice often exceeded, that of the Hebrew scriptures. And that is why Christians today treat those same writings with reverence. As the second letter of Peter, probably written after the apostolic era, put it, 'men and women moved by the Holy Spirit spoke from God' (1:21).

For the disciples in the upper room, the significance of the words was intensely personal rather than a matter of future church doctrine. Jesus their teacher was leaving them, but he was promising them a 'new' teacher, another rabbi... and this teacher would be none other than the Holy Spirit of God.

Perhaps this was an element of the 'peace' that Jesus now left with them. It was not, he said, peace as the world gives it. The world's peace is more often than not achieved by conquest, like the *Pax Romana* which ruled the Roman Empire of the time. That was indeed peace of a kind, as is the peace of compromise or of abject surrender. But none of these gets anywhere near the sense of the word *shalom*, which Jesus would have used. *Shalom* is wholeness: it is nothing less than a state of union with God, with our surroundings and with ourselves. Conquest, compromise and surrender, in their different ways, cannot create that kind of peace.

But Jesus can, and does. At this moment the disciples would not, we imagine, have felt very peaceful, yet more tranquil waters did lie ahead. After all, it was 'Peace' that Jesus gave them in this same room on the evening of the resurrection (John 20:19) when he breathed the same Holy Spirit into their nostrils. It was 'peace', Paul says, which he made 'through the blood of his cross' (Colossians 1:20). The peace of Christ is the peace achieved by sacrifice rather than surrender, and by love rather than conquest. As the disciples sat spellbound around him, it was that peace which their master bequeathed to them as his parting gift. It was that peace which enabled him to urge them not to let their hearts be troubled (an echo of the opening words of this chapter) nor to 'let them be afraid'.

If the world's peace is simply absence of conflict, what unique gift can Christians bring to help the search for a deeper and more profound peace? What is the connection between social and international peace and what we might call 'inward' peace—being at one with God, our circumstances and ourselves?

GOING TO THE FATHER

'You heard me say to you, "I am going away, and I am coming to you." If you loved me, you would rejoice that I am going to the Father, because the Father is greater than I. And now I have told you this before it occurs, so that when it does occur, you may believe. I will no longer talk much with you, for the ruler of this world is coming. He has no power over me; but I do as the Father has commanded me, so that the world may know that I love the Father. Rise, let us be on our way.'

JOHN 14:28–31

Indeed, the disciples *had* heard Jesus say that he was going away, but they had hardly seen that as a cause for rejoicing. Yet Jesus pointed out to them how selfish an attitude that was. For him, it was a matter of joy that he was returning 'to the Father' —going back 'home', as one might say.

John is more aware than the other Evangelists of Jesus as a 'visitor' from another place. Right from the prologue of the Gospel, he has seen the incarnation in terms of a limited and temporary 'exercise', in which the Word, Jesus, 'pitched his tent among us' (1:14, literally). The events of this Passover evening had begun with Jesus knowing that he 'had come from God and was going to God' (13:3). The earthy rabbi of Matthew, Mark and Luke is, for John, the true light of God coming into the world and taking flesh, not an alien so much as a divine visitor.

The disciples struggled with such ideas, understandably. It was not until after the resurrection and Pentecost that they began to understand something of the implications of all this. It was later, much later, that the beloved disciple could say, 'We have seen his glory, as of the Father's only Son, full of grace and truth' (John 1:14).

So Jesus's rebuke is gentle: 'If you loved me, you would rejoice that I am going to the Father.' Yes, of course they would, if they could only get their minds round the whole idea. But they would have had less problem with his next words than some Christians have done: '...because the Father is greater than I'. To these devout Jews it would have seemed little other than stating the obvious, for the Lord God, Yahweh, the God of Abraham, Isaac and Jacob, was infinite and eternal, the creator of the ends of the earth. *Of course* he was 'greater' than Jesus. Indeed, this statement may have softened slightly their shock at his earlier claim that 'whoever has seen me has seen the Father' (14:9). For Christians trying to sort out their Christology, however, there may appear to be some degree of contradiction there.

In fact, there is a splendid consistency about the way in which this Gospel speaks of the nature of Jesus. All through the Gospel, it reiterates, time and again, that he has not come to do his own will but 'the will of him who sent me'. Here, in this very passage, he explains that he does what 'the Father has commanded'. Only the greater can give 'commands' to the lesser, but in this case it is a matter of rank or function rather than fundamental nature.

John is clear that Jesus not only represents the Father but manifests him to the world. He is 'God the only Son, who is close to the Father's heart' and consequently has 'made him known' (1:18). His obedience on earth to his Father's will is a mark not of his subservience but of his unity with the Father. They are, as it were, 'of one mind'. In any case, the writer of this Gospel really leaves us in no doubt that Jesus shares the

Father's divine nature. His opening sentence settles any argument: 'The Word [Jesus] was with God, and the Word was God' (1:1).

Jesus, then, wanted his disciples to share in his joy in doing the Father's will, but he was also aware, and wanted them to know for future reference, that an hour of darkness was at hand. 'The ruler of this world is coming'—though he has no power over Jesus.

This mysterious figure is unique to John's writings. Others speak of Satan, the Adversary, the one who opposes the will of God, or of the Devil. For this writer, the 'god of this world' is the personification of the ungodly world that surrounded them, a figure whose power derives from the evil choices which had led society to live as though there were no true God. He flourishes in that barren wilderness of wilful unbelief.

But, Jesus assured his followers, 'he has no power over me'. The one who has put his faith totally in the Father is immune to the powers of this anti-god, who can only flourish where faith is absent. Jesus was the perfect example of such trust and submission, and so he was impervious to the plans and schemes of the 'god of this world'. Such a 'god' could invoke darkness and suffering, and for a time it might even appear that he had won a kind of victory. But it was not a final victory. That rested with the will of the Father.

Jesus told them this in words that must have seemed both baffling and bewildering, but with the purpose of eventual enlightenment—'so that when it does occur, you may believe'. These were, in fact, his last words in this particular setting.

The meal was over. The scene was set. Perhaps the night was hot and the air heavy. At any rate, at that moment it would appear that the proceedings were interrupted. 'Rise, let us be on our way.' The discourse was not over, but the rest of it would be set against another scene and in another place.

Christians have had many different images of Satan. Is the one here —of the 'prince of this world'—a more helpful one for an age that has problems with a personal Devil? Here are no horns or forked tail, but the personification of a secular, God-denying spirit. Would our contemporaries recognize the reality of that?

GRAFTED TO THE VINE

'I am the true vine, and my Father is the vinegrower. He removes every branch in me that bears no fruit. Every branch that bears fruit he prunes to make it bear more fruit. You have already been cleansed by the word that I have spoken to you. Abide in me as I abide in you. Just as the branch cannot bear fruit by itself unless it abides in the vine, neither can you unless you abide in me.'

JOHN 15:1–4

It's not clear where the disciples went after leaving the upper room. Probably they headed towards the garden of Gethsemane, which is presumably the 'garden' ('olive grove', NIV) identified later as their destination (18:1). On the other hand, they may have done no more than move outdoors to a courtyard or garden at the house itself. Late April is very pleasant in Jerusalem, generally warm and with a spring-like flavour about it.

After several hours indoors, they might equally well have chosen to stroll through the quiet streets, slowly making their way across the city, eventually crossing the Kidron valley and climbing up one of the paths towards the Mount of Olives. Jesus may have spoken as they walked—something he seems to have done on a number of occasions (see, for instance, Mark 8:27). Archbishop William Temple, among others, seemed to favour the idea that they were making their way across the temple courts.

The vine was, and had been for centuries, a familiar image of

Israel. God had planted and watered it, and looked for fruit from his chosen and cherished people. Sadly he was too often disappointed—a great theme of the Hebrew prophets. Now Jesus gave a new significance to the image: he himself was the vine, the Father was the one who had planted and nurtured it, and his people were its branches. In other words, God now had a new vine, bearing new fruit, and a new people, dependent on his Son.

Jesus is the *true* vine. That is the emphasis here. The old, unreliable, unfaithful, unproductive vine had been replaced. He is in himself the new Israel, and he will gather his people, whom he describes as the 'branches' of the tree. The Father, however, is still its founder and keeper, and he tends his vine with patient attention, cutting away the dead wood and 'pruning' (the word carries the sense of 'purifying') the fruitful branches so that they produce more and more.

It's interesting that here there are two kinds of surgery, as it were. One is simply to purge what is dead and useless. The other is to promote growth and health. It may well be that the same knife or saw would be used for both, but the objectives are almost diametrically opposite. Sometimes we have to ask ourselves, when we encounter God's painful dealings with us, into which of these categories they fall. Is this the purging away of something intrinsically evil, or is it the surgical removal of something that hinders a closer walk and a more fruitful discipleship?

At any rate, the process takes place. Jesus assured his friends that they were already 'cleansed' by the word he had spoken to them. This repeats what he had told them after the foot-washing: 'You are clean.' But now he doesn't have to add the terrible words, '…though not all of you'. For Judas, the other kind of pruning has taken place, the kind that removes dead branches.

Now the branches, pruned and ready to bear fruit, have one overriding responsibility, and that is to stay connected to the tree. Branches detached from the trunk cannot survive, let alone be fruitful. In the same way, the disciples of Jesus cannot survive or produce fruit unless they remain 'in him'. The word 'remain' is one with which this Gospel has already made us familiar, most accurately translated as 'abide'. It has the sense of 'making a home' or establishing a residence—Jesus wanted his followers, then and now, to 'abide' in him, to make him the fixed and permanent base for living. Just as the branch can produce nothing while separated from the vine, so to try to live a Christian life while separated from Christ is a lost cause. The branch must 'abide' in the vine, but the 'vine' promises to 'abide' in the branches. It is a two-way process, with the branch contributing to the growth of the tree, and the tree making the growth of the branch possible. The technical name for this process in living organisms is 'symbiosis', and it is as good a picture of the true Christian life as we are likely to find.

If the Church is, as Paul calls it, the 'body of Christ' (1 Corinthians 12:27), then we can also think of it as the vine of which individual Christians are branches. That suggests that the most dangerous thing for a Christian to do is wilfully to be separated from the Church. Yet constantly we find that when people get into difficulties, especially when they feel they have failed in some way, they 'separate' themselves from the one sure source of strength, forgiveness and hope. If they do, they are in danger of ending up like the separated, dead branches of a tree, devoid of life and slowly losing even the outward appearance of a living branch. It may be hard to accept, but isn't the gardener's pruning knife preferable to the rake that gathers up the dead leaves and branches for the rubbish tip?

Of one thing we can be sure: there is no real life separated from the vine.

The metaphor of Jesus as the vine and his disciples as branches raises the question: in what ways can and should the life of the Christian draw on the life of the vine? How can the 'branches' stay connected?

BEARING FRUIT

'I am the vine, you are the branches. Those who abide in me and I in them bear much fruit, because apart from me you can do nothing. Whoever does not abide in me is thrown away like a branch and withers; such branches are gathered, thrown into the fire, and burned. If you abide in me, and my words abide in you, ask for whatever you wish, and it will be done for you. My Father is glorified by this, that you bear much fruit and become my disciples.'

JOHN 15:5–8

The discourse on the vine continues, but with a slightly different emphasis. First Jesus asserted that he was the vine and his Father the vine grower. That established a fundamental truth, that the vine under discussion belongs to God. He planted it, tends it and the fruit will be his. This is entirely in keeping with the whole tenor of Christ's teaching in John's Gospel. He was on earth to do the will of his Father and to 'complete his work'. The vine, the new people of God, the source of blessing ('fruit') for the whole world, is the Father's.

But Jesus is the vine itself. If William Temple was right in setting this scene on the disciples' way to the Mount of Olives by moonlight, then they would have seen as they passed through the temple courtyard a striking carving of a vine draped across the gateway, as a constant reminder to the people of Israel of their calling as God's vine. Sadly, as a nation they had failed that calling. Now, in the coming of the Messiah, Jesus, the old imagery is to be renewed. *He* is the vine now, the embodiment of the presence and purpose of God.

'You are the branches': the rest of this passage is the unpacking of this metaphor. Most simply, the 'you' refers to those who are, or will be, 'my disciples'. So the branches of the vine are the followers of Jesus the Messiah, those who sit at his feet and hang on his words, those who are made 'clean by the word' and set out to show their love for him by obedience to his 'commandments'.

That is the practical, visible definition of a 'branch' of the vine. But there is a deeper and more mystical one, which Jesus unfolds to them in a kind of word-play on the theme of 'abiding'. This deserves close attention, because it would seem to be at the heart of the whole relationship between Jesus and anyone who seeks to be his 'disciple'.

First there is the word 'abide' itself. For obvious reasons— notably that it's not one we use much in modern England— most translations prefer to render it as 'remain'. However, the NRSV (wisely, in my view) keeps to the slightly archaic 'abide', presumably because it conveys more accurately the flavour of the Greek word *meno*. It carries the notion of rest, of dwelling, of residence even. The two disciples on the road to Emmaus memorably invited Jesus to 'abide with us, because night is falling', in other words, 'Stay at our house' (Luke 24:29). And earlier on this very evening Jesus had assured his followers that in his Father's house there were many 'abiding places'—places to rest, to reside, to find company and refreshment.

To 'abide', then, is to make one's dwelling, and that was what Jesus both offered and invited his disciples to do. And as they made their dwelling in him, he offered to make his dwelling in them. It is a mutual *in-dwelling*. Although it is the Christian who is 'commanded' to abide in Christ, the inevitable consequence is that Christ will abide in the Christian. This is not, as Temple points out, presented as 'occasion and consequence, but as a two-fold condition which we are bidden to bring into existence'.

Put more simply, the truth is unavoidable. The Christian life is about the mystery of the relationship between the Saviour and the believer, and that relationship is based on the principle of 'abiding'. We 'abide' in Jesus; he 'abides' in us. He makes his home in our lives; our lives find their home in him. In the end, the issue is never about rules and regulations, but about relationship: 'he in us, and we in him'. And the relationship is effective because of this mutuality. He abides and we abide.

This also tells us something about the fellowship in which eternal life is to be found. It is the fellowship of the vine. The life of the vine comes from outside itself (from God, the vine grower) but is carried into the whole tree, which is Christ. In that tree those who believe in him, his 'disciples', are 'branches', drawing their life from the vine just as the vine draws its life from the soil. But Jesus didn't say that he is the trunk and we are the branches, because that would be to imply that there is some division between branch and tree. The whole tree, trunk *and* branches, is the vine, just as, in the teaching of the apostle Paul, it is the whole body, head and limbs and organs, that makes up the Church, the body of Christ (see 1 Corinthians 12:12, 27).

That is why we should always think of Christianity in collective rather than individualistic terms. 'I [Jesus] am the vine, you [disciples, all of you] are the branches'—not so much individually as together. And together with Jesus we are the new and mystical vine, the 'Israel of God', created and destined to produce fruit and be a blessing to the whole world.

All of this flows from the relationship of 'abiding', which is also the secret of effective prayer. Those who abide in Jesus, and in whom his words abide, may ask for 'whatever you wish', and 'it will be done for you'. As we have already seen, true prayer is co-operation with the purpose of God. Within the vine, that co-operation reaches completeness, as the words of Jesus dwell

—make their home—in the hearts of the believers, and the believers dwell—make their homes—in Christ.

There is a perfect congruence of intention here, and no room for difference. The branches don't argue with the tree! And in that perfect congruence, prayer becomes naturally and normally a commitment to the divine purpose: 'Your will be done, your kingdom come.' That is the prayer that is always answered. Although it is indeed 'whatever you wish', it is also and always what the vine and the vine grower intend. That kind of prayer is irresistible.

In this way, the vine bears its fruit. The nourishment it draws from the soil is conveyed to the branches and in due course becomes fruit to bless the world. And the credit goes to the vine-grower! 'My Father is glorified by this, that you bear much fruit and become [perhaps, more helpfully, 'show yourselves to be'] my disciples.'

That is the glory of the vine—its fruit. The wood of the vine, as Ezekiel once pointed out, is of very little value (15:2–4). Its glory is the grape. It is as the vine grower, the tree and the branches work together, with a unity of purpose, that those who pass by point at it and say, 'What a splendid vine!'

In what practical, daily ways could the modern Christian deepen this sense of abiding in Christ? And what difference might it make to our witness in the world and our life of prayer?

COMPLETE JOY

'As the Father has loved me, so I have loved you; abide in my love.
If you keep my commandments, you will abide in my love, just as
I have kept my Father's commandments and abide in his love. I
have said these things to you so that my joy may be in you, and that
your joy may be complete. This is my commandment, that you
love one another as I have loved you.'

JOHN 15:9–12

This passage introduces two new themes, joy and love—though
'love', of course, has already figured largely in the discourse.
Now the principle of abiding is broadened, however, to include
the notion of abiding in Christ's love, and of his joy abiding in
the disciple.

Jesus had already mentioned his commandment to them to
'love one another'. Now he was to give it fresh impetus. Just as
they were to abide in him, and to abide in the vine, so they were
to abide in his *love*, to find their place of security in it. And the
particular kind of love is carefully defined: it is a love modelled
on the Father's love for his Son, and his Son's love for them.
That is the quality of love in which they are to 'abide'. What are
its distinctive characteristics?

It's well known that the word Jesus used here for 'love' is
agape, in classical Greek the highest and noblest form of love,
to be distinguished from *eros* (sexual love) and *philadelphia*
(brotherly love). As Christ and the apostles were to use it, it

expressed love of a self-giving, sacrificial kind, utterly unselfish, demanding nothing in return—love not for the lovely but for the beloved. This, as Jesus was shortly to explain, was the quality of love that his own life would demonstrate to the ultimate on Golgotha. But it was also the love that led the Father to give his Son for the salvation of 'the world', the unbelieving, God-rejecting *cosmos*. This is a love far beyond sentiment or even 'feelings', a love that reflects the very nature of God himself, who *is* Love (1 John 4:16).

Possibly the modern world, with its emphasis on self-fulfilment and the pursuit of happiness, might find this definition of love difficult. In the Anglican marriage service I am always moved when the couple exchange rings, because the words they address to each other are of quite revolutionary import to contemporary ears. The world's idea of love could often be expressed like this: 'I love you, I want you, and I'm going to have you.' But here, in the midst of this happy occasion, a man and a woman look at each other and say exactly the opposite: 'All that I am I give to you, and all that I have I share with you.' In doing that, they are expressing *agape* love, and that is the kind of love in which Jesus urged his disciples to 'make their home'. If the disciples were to abide in the love of Jesus they would be making such love the foundation of their lives, their 'dwelling-place'. It was a thought that Jesus gently developed as the evening wore on.

But it was not a command without reward. It was given to them with a simple purpose: that they might know his 'joy'. The word *kara* means gladness, rejoicing, even bliss, so this was much more than some temporary lift of the spirits or moment of euphoria. Jesus exhibited this 'joy' in his life, even at moments of testing and opposition. It may well be the very quality that people found most attractive about him, compared to the dour and pious Pharisees and teachers of the law. Now he invited his disciples and, with them, all in later ages who were to believe in him, to abide in his love so that his joy may abide in them, and their joy be 'complete'.

This must have seemed something of a paradox to the disciples. So far, what they had got from the farewell discourse was the sombre news that Jesus was leaving them very soon, though sending them a slightly mysterious Helper, and that this was the hour of the prince of this world, which sounded rather ominous. Yet now they were being told that 'joy' was to be their reward, and not just any joy—'*my* joy', the joy that lit up the life of Christ. This joy would completely fill them: that is the sense of 'complete' here. It would be an all-encompassing experience of delight and gladness.

This was a theme to which Jesus would later return. For the present, the emphasis is undoubtedly on the keeping of 'my commandments'. This doesn't refer to rules or laws, of course, but to the specific commands he was now giving to them. Again the analogy is with his own unswerving obedience to his Father's commands. The joy that Jesus knew and demonstrated in his life flowed from the fact that he lived it according to the Father's will. It was that which gave Jesus his tremendous sense of purpose. He knew where he had come from, and he knew where he was going. In that certainty he knew that he was abiding in the Father's love, and in that love was his 'joy'. Now he wanted to let his disciples into the secret of the fulfilled and happy life—simple obedience to the divine will. He had found it, and he wanted to share it with them. If they kept his commands, they would abide in his love, just as he kept his Father's commands and dwelt in his love. And from that would flow inevitably the same joy that Jesus knew, the joy of a fulfilled purpose.

It's a commonplace of human experience that satisfaction comes from work successfully completed. The artist takes pleasure from the finished painting, the carpenter from the finely turned chair, the teacher from the pupil who has made the lesson their own. Here the experience is lifted to a higher plane. To share, even in a small way, in God's great purposes is to experience the true joy of fulfilment.

We live in a society which believes that it is very good at enjoying itself, but seems to find 'joy', in this deeper sense, rather elusive. Are there clues in these words of Jesus to a more satisfying experience of joy? What might it mean in practice?

True friendship

'This is my commandment, that you love one another as I have loved you. No one has greater love than this, to lay down one's life for one's friends. You are my friends if you do what I command you. I do not call you servants any longer, because the servant does not know what the master is doing; but I have called you friends, because I have made known to you everything that I have heard from my Father. You did not choose me but I chose you. And I appointed you to go and bear fruit, fruit that will last, so that the Father will give you whatever you ask him in my name. I am giving you these commands so that you may love one another.'

JOHN 15:12–17

On Remembrance Sunday in November every year, at thousands upon thousands of war memorials up and down Britain, the dead of two World Wars are remembered. Often a sentence from this passage is also read; indeed it is often engraved somewhere on the memorial, in the words of the King James Version: 'Greater love hath no man than this, that a man lay down his life for his friends.' As we commemorate those who 'laid down their lives', we also recognize that there is no greater form of sacrifice. To die for a person, or for a cause, is to demonstrate the ultimate in commitment.

Of course, it is a little unrealistic to think of all those young men and women who died in war as 'laying down their lives'. They didn't *want* to die—why should they? In many cases their lives were not so much 'laid down' as cruelly snatched from them, by bomb, bullet, fire or shell. Yet we *can* say the words, and mean them, because theirs was a 'sacrifice' in the sense that they considered the cause for which they were fighting, the homes and families which they saw themselves as defending, as worth this great price. We own nothing more valuable than our own lives, and to lay them on the line for a cause, or for another person, is the greatest sacrifice that we can make.

So these are familiar words, even to many people who don't know that they were spoken by Jesus or are taken from the Bible. They are respected because they express a universally recognized truth—the ultimate proof of love. We are all aware that this is not just theory, either. Mothers have died for their children, husbands for their wives, sisters for brothers, friends for friends. Sacrificial love *is* the highest form of love, beyond dispute. That was the point that Jesus was making here to his disciples.

Yet the fact is that these words are engraved on memorials and read at Remembrance Day services out of their true context. Because they do express a universal truth there is no great harm in that, but the quotation invariably ends with the phrase 'for one's friends', which excludes the following words: 'You are my friends if you do what I command you.' Jesus was making an intensely personal statement of commitment. If there is no greater love than that which lays down its life for someone, then he wanted the disciples to know that in laying down his life for them he would be proving the full extent of his love for them. For—and this is the point—*they* were his friends. This motley little band of fishermen, tax collectors, political agitators and farmers were the friends for whom he was about to die, provided they did what he commanded them. He reminded them what it was that he had commanded them—to love one another with the same quality of love as he had loved them.

So Jesus set love firmly in the context of sacrifice, of self-giving. He was soon to 'lay down his life' for his friends—and of course not only these 'friends' but all those through human history who were to become his friends. As Paul pointed out, the sacrifice is even more momentous than that, because when Jesus made it, those people who would be its beneficiaries down the centuries, including Christians living today, were *not yet* his friends. This is how Paul put it: 'Rarely will anyone die for a righteous person—though perhaps for a good person someone might actually dare to die. But God proves his love for us in that while we were still sinners Christ died for us' (Romans 5:7–8). 'While we were still sinners' Jesus gave his life for us, so that we might *become* his friends.

These men were already his friends, although one among them would shortly deny it, asserting that he did not even *know* Jesus. They were more than 'servants' (the actual word is 'slaves') because servants merely carry out commands without knowing the master's intentions. But to this chosen group he had begun, and would eventually complete, a process of spiritual enlightenment which would make them privy not only to the will of Jesus, but also to the will of the Father himself. No 'servants' would be so privileged. Only valued and trusted friends would be admitted into the privy council of the will of God—and that was to be their great privilege.

But it is the privilege of every Christian, no matter how humble, uneducated or unconsidered in the world's eyes, to be a 'friend' of Jesus, because every Christian is what they are only because he laid down his life for them. Without that sacrifice, made on the cross, our sins would be unforgiven, death would remain victorious and the gates of heaven would be closed to us. So much hung on that single act of obedience to the Father's will, that sacrifice of love, that it can truly be seen as the turning point of human history. By one supreme demonstration of 'no greater love' the Saviour made people no better than we are his friends.

It was love that led him to Golgotha, not a stern sense of duty or a reluctant obedience to the sternly imposed will of the

Father. As ever, the Trinity was of one mind, united in purpose and love. 'God so loved the world that he gave his only Son' (3:16) and the Son so loved us that he 'laid down his life' for these as-yet-unknown friends. This is a glorious conspiracy of love, with its goal the blessing of the whole world.

But it also lays a responsibility on those who benefit from it. There's no doubt that many an act of sacrificial love has failed in its ultimate intention, often because those for whom it was made failed to respond to it. Beyond doubt, many of the men who died in the carnage of the Great War believed that they were risking their lives in a war 'to end wars'. At least, that was what they were told. Yet 21 years after it ended, Europe—having apparently learned nothing from their sacrifice—was to do it all again. While professing to honour their memory and value their sacrifice, it seemed to be quite lightly set aside. Surely love that pays the ultimate price demands the ultimate response?

Even if that is seldom entirely true in the world of hard politics and pragmatism, it must apply in the world of the spirit. The sacrificial love of Jesus was intended to bear fruit, 'fruit that will last', in the lives of his 'friends', those chosen by him to fulfil his command to preach and practise love in the world of their day. It was to become visible in the life of the early Church as these very disciples carried the message and the example of saving love to the world. But it is the task of Christians in every age to follow their example. Sacrificial love requires of us nothing less.

We have not 'chosen' Christ, but he has 'chosen' us. What does that mean in our own experience? Is it a mark of our journey of faith? And in what ways does he 'appoint' us to bear 'fruit that will last'? What would that 'fruit' be?

18

THE WORLD'S OPPOSITION

'If the world hates you, be aware that it hated me before it hated
you. If you belonged to the world, the world would love you as its
own. Because you do not belong to the world, but I have chosen
you out of the world—therefore the world hates you. Remember
the word that I said to you, "Servants are not greater than their
master." If they persecuted me, they will persecute you; if they
kept my word, they will keep yours also. But they will do all these
things to you on account of my name, because they do not know
him who sent me.'

JOHN 15:18–21

Having called the disciples to love each other, Jesus warned
them that conversely the 'world' would hate them, just as it had
hated him. These words introduce a theme that runs through
the rest of the discourse, striking a sombre note about what lay
ahead for them after his departure. It's not uncommon in such
farewell speeches to issue warnings, of course: the leader is
naturally anxious that his work should not be undone by his
enemies, who might well be simply waiting to spoil things once
he has left the scene. Probably, by the time the fourth Gospel
was written, well after the first wave of persecutions of the
Church, hints that Jesus had given about future trials would
have assumed a far greater relevance.

Certainly it was true that the first Christians were marked
men and women—not necessarily 'hated', at first, but treated

with suspicion and contempt by the authorities while generally, it would seem, respected by the ordinary people. Later that suspicion hardened into serious opposition, as it became clear that the 'Jesus Movement' was not minded to evaporate, as so many cults and sects in Judaism had done, but had the potential to become a genuine threat to the established religious and political order. The 'common people' for the most part came to accept the official line that the Christians were blasphemers, or a kind of political fifth column. Yet at the same time, that very 'difference' between the Christians and everybody else served to attract many people to the Church, even in times of persecution. It must be true, they felt, if these men and women were ready to die for it.

Jesus expressed this division in terms of a conflict between the values of the 'world' and the values of the Kingdom. That conflict is inevitably present, provided the Church is being faithful to its radical message. Periods were to follow in history when the Church and secular society went far beyond neutral co-existence and became twin pillars of the establishment. In those circumstances the only people persecuted were those who challenged the political-religious established order.

But that lay far beyond the present and the immediate future for the first disciples. For the first three centuries of its existence, the Church was constantly the target of cruel and systematic persecution, and the more faithful it was to the message of Jesus the more wholehearted were the attempts to stamp it out. No wonder the Christians clung to these words of Jesus, which provided at least an explanation of the hatred and abuse they experienced, and compared that abuse to the hatred that eventually led Jesus himself to the cross.

It was all, Jesus said, a question of allegiance. You don't 'belong' to the 'world', that God-rejecting social order. You belong to God, and that very allegiance is a constant rebuke to those who have chosen to reject it. 'Servants are not greater than their master.' Indeed, they are always destined to suffer the same fate if they remain loyal to him. The Christians would suffer then, as many continue suffering to this day, 'on account of my name'—for bearing witness to the name of Jesus. Modern martyrs bear testimony to this truth—Janani Luwum in Uganda under Amin, Oscar Romero in El Salvador, Christians in China during the Cultural Revolution, believers who died 'for the Name' in Rwanda, the Sudan, the old Soviet Union and many other places over the last century. It was not that they provoked opposition or set out to overthrow governments or dictators, but that remaining faithful to Christ bore for them a terrible cost.

This opposition was not, as Jesus saw it, simply a matter of personal dislike or animosity. It had deep spiritual roots. It happened 'because they do not know him who sent me'. It was not so much that they failed to understand that Jesus was God's divine agent (one could put that down to misunderstanding or ignorance) but that they did not know God at all. If they had had a true 'knowledge' of God they would have recognized the marks of God in the works of Christ and of his followers.

So, for Jesus, opposition, then and later, was not a political or religious matter but a sign of spiritual unbelief. No one who recognized the authority of God would treat Christ, or his followers, with spite, malice and abuse.

It is sometimes hard for us to see beyond the outward behaviour of an individual or group to its spiritual roots. Time and again in our own society people deplore what they call 'anti-social' behaviour, or complain that 'things aren't what they used to be'. They tend to blame schools, or parents, or the Church, or the government—or all four! Yet the truth is that behaviour springs from what Jesus called 'the heart' (Matthew 15:18–20), from the deep wellspring of our personality, where our values and beliefs are formed and nourished.

Jesus asked his disciples to look more deeply at the motives of those who opposed him and would soon oppose them. It was their fundamental allegiance that was faulty. They 'belonged to the world'. They owed their loyalties to its corrupt goals, its flawed systems and its selfish ambitions. In other words, they lived as though God didn't exist—or, in the language of this discourse, as though the god who *does* exist and holds sway is the 'god of this world'.

That is why all of our social problems are at heart spiritual ones. The first priority of a healthy society is to dethrone its false gods. But—as Jesus teaches here—that is a costly and painful process.

If we accept this analysis of evil, what can the Church do beyond deploring it and putting up fences around the 'holy places'? How could our own society begin to accept that its problems are not at heart economic, political or cultural but spiritual?

FINDING THE TRUTH

19

GUILTY OF HATRED

'If I had not come and spoken to them, they would not have sin; but now they have no excuse for their sin. Whoever hates me hates my Father also. If I had not done among them the works that no one else did, they would not have sin. But now they have seen and hated both me and my Father. It was to fulfil the word that is written in their law, "They hated me without a cause."'

JOHN 15:22–25

Jesus had already made the point that 'the world' had failed to 'know God'. Presumably this referred to the whole unbelieving world system, humankind in its pride and emptiness without faith. Now, it seems, he turns his attention to a more specific target, those who had heard him and seen his 'works'—in other words, the Jewish contemporaries of Jesus.

The Gospel began with the reminder that Jesus had come to those who were 'his own' (1:11). That may well carry a double meaning—those who were 'his own' by race and kinship, and those who were God's 'own' by call and covenant, the people he had chosen 'out of all the families of the earth' (Amos 3:6). But sadly 'his own did not receive him' (John 1:11). Apart from the handful of his followers, and the minority of Jews who later believed and were baptized, the people of the covenant failed to recognize or receive their Messiah. That is not a statement of racial criticism, much less anti-Semitic, but simply a fact of history. The Jewish people of the time of Jesus did not accept his Messiahship. Indeed, some of them, possibly a minority, went beyond that and actually sought to destroy him. As it is put here, in words from the Psalms, 'They hated me without a cause' (Psalms 35:19; 69:4).

The words of Jesus put the case in its starkest terms. Unlike the rest of the unbelieving 'world', the Jewish people of his time had been the recipients of a unique and extraordinary revelation. They had heard his words and seen his 'signs'. That, however, was the measure of their sin, for this was not the sin of ignorance but of wilful rejection. Jesus put it twice in almost identical terms. If he had not spoken to them the words of God, they would not be guilty of sin. And if he had not done in their presence works which no one else had ever done, they would also not be guilty of sin. But he had, and they were. It is a fearful indictment, summarized here as having 'seen and *hated* both me and my Father'.

It is important to read these words in both their biblical and historical context. The Jews to whom Jesus referred were, of course, the Jews of that time. It would be totally wrong to apply his words to Jewish people at other times, especially our own contemporaries. It is probable that Jesus had in mind the temple hierarchy in particular. They seem to have been the people who stirred up hatred against him and brought about his arrest and execution.

Historically speaking, this Gospel was probably written when the dispute between the fast-growing Christian Church and the Jewish authorities had become bitter and angry. Cruel and vicious things were said on both sides, as Jewish believers in Jesus were expelled from synagogues and Christian leaders denounced the Jewish religion in extreme and often abusive terms. That is the historical setting, and we need to understand how the early Church was anxious to find anything in the teaching of Jesus which would justify the stand they were taking.

The constant reference to 'the Jews' in this Gospel is baffling without that understanding of its context, because the beloved disciple was clearly himself a devout Jew, as were all the apostles and also, of course, Jesus himself. In other words, just as 'the world' must be defined as 'that part of human society which lives as though there were no God', so 'the Jews' must be defined as 'those members of the covenant people of God who consciously rejected the Messiah'.

However, these words of Jesus raise a more general truth, which applies to all of us and at all times. There is judgment as well as blessing in knowledge. That's to say, just as it is not really possible to sin in ignorance (because if you genuinely didn't know that it was wrong, you couldn't be blamed for doing it), so knowledge of the truth judges us. We can no longer 'plead ignorance'. The coming of Jesus, his words of crystal truth, his acts and signs of power and love, were a blessing to those who received them *and a judgment on those who didn't*. That is a sobering thought. It means that to have heard and seen *and then rejected* is the most perilous of all spiritual conditions. Here, it was the fate of some of those living at the time of the incarnation. Now it may be the peril of those who have had the blessing of a knowledge of the truth but have then consciously and wilfully rejected it.

All sin is sin against conscience. That is recognized. But the greater problem, which seems to be at the heart of what Jesus is saying about those who hate him and hate the Father, is the sin of the 'darkened conscience', which occurs when a person's conscience itself has been so corrupted or distorted that it sees white instead of black and black instead of white. If the conscience determines whether an act is sinful or not, then obviously things are desperate for the person whose conscience itself is faulty. Rather like a malfunctioning computer on an aircraft's navigational system, its 'signals' will be misleading.

The only way to avoid the danger of a corrupted or darkened conscience is to bring it constantly to the source of right judgment, which is the truth of God. Perhaps that ought to be qualified as 'the truth of God to the best of our understanding', because our perception of truth, unlike God's, is always partial, at any rate until that day when we shall 'know fully, as we are fully known' (1 Corinthians 13:12). Like a car being subjected to its regular roadworthiness check, that test alone will determine whether our conscience is still a reliable guide.

The problem for these unbelieving 'Jews', for example, was not primarily one of misunderstanding or ignorance, but of a distorted conscience: 'They hated me *without a cause*.' And hating him, they also hated the Father, because the two are an indissoluble unity. In that kind of darkness, there can be no light.

However, there are no grounds here for any feelings of moral superiority. What was true in that particular instance is true always and everywhere: privilege brings responsibilities. And there has never been a greater privilege than the gospel of Christ. Of those to whom much is given, much will be required. It is a challenging thought.

Do these words of Jesus really mean that it would be better to remain in ignorance of the great blessings of the gospel—'better' in the sense that to know its truth is to be deprived of excuse for disbelief? Or are they rather a challenge to the Christian to be sure to live out to the full its obligations as well as enjoying its privileges?

20

THE ADVOCATE

'When the Advocate comes, whom I will send to you from the Father, the Spirit of truth who comes from the Father, he will testify on my behalf. You also are to testify because you have been with me from the beginning.'

JOHN 15:26–27

Jesus now directed his disciples' attention to a further implication in the title 'Paraclete'. This does indeed mean 'Helper', and they may well have felt that at that moment they needed all the help they could get. But in a specialized sense it also means 'Advocate'—the lawyer or counsel who appears 'for' a defendant in a court of law and argues his or her case for them.

Perhaps in the light of all this talk about opposition and disbelief, Jesus now set out to show them that the 'case' they were to take with them into the unbelieving world was a sound one, and supported by a powerful 'Counsellor' or Advocate. Indeed, he would have divine rather than earthly credentials, granted to him by the Father, no less, though he would be sent to them by Jesus himself: 'whom I will send to you from the Father'.

For Christians in later ages, that apparently small detail (the role of the Son in the sending of the Spirit from the Father) was to become a point of bitter controversy. The Nicene Creed, in the form used by the Churches of the West, including the Roman Catholics, Anglicans, Lutherans and all the major Free

Churches, speaks of the Holy Spirit 'proceeding from the Father *and the Son*'. The Eastern Orthodox Churches, feeling that such a claim detracts from the sovereignty of God, use the same Creed but omit the phrase about the Son—what is known as the *filioque* clause ('and the Son' in Latin). In that infuriating way whereby doctrines that are meant to unite end up dividing, this apparently minor difference has helped to keep great swathes of Christendom apart for centuries.

However, none of this would have been in the minds of the disciples at the time. Probably for them it was a great reassurance to know that this rather mysterious 'Advocate' would be sent to them by Jesus himself, though, as was soon to be made clear, there was no differentiation of purpose between the Father and the Son. The Advocate would be their gift to the Church.

Already in this Gospel we have seen Jesus in dispute with the religious teachers of his day. This was a major theme of chapters 5—8. There, too, he had called as evidence the 'works' that he had done, as proof that the Father had sent him. In that way, Jesus had claimed, his Father had 'testified on my behalf' (5:37). Now all of this 'evidence', this testimony, was to be presented to the world and argued with persuasion by the Advocate who would be sent to his followers.

This Advocate also bears another very significant title. He is the 'Spirit of truth'—the 'truthful Spirit', perhaps in contrast to the 'lying spirit' who is the god of this world. Not every legal advocate always speaks all of the truth, needless to say. Sometimes the defence counsel will know that their client is guilty, but will at the very least collude in attempts to cloud the issue and secure a 'not guilty' verdict. But God's Advocate is the Spirit of truth. Nothing *but* truth can come from him. What he would tell them would be true, and what he told the world would be true also, whether it was believed or not.

So God had witnessed to the authority of Jesus, and in future the Holy Spirit would also testify to the truth about him. But at this point Jesus added another promise: 'You also are to testify.'

The disciples themselves, anxious and troubled as they were at that moment, were in fact to be crucial witnesses in what we may call 'the case for Jesus'. You could do this, he told them 'because you have been with me from the beginning'.

That was to be the fundamental definition of an apostle—an eye-witness of the event. We find it in the prologue to Luke's Gospel, where he writes that he will set down an 'orderly account of the events that have been fulfilled among us, just as they were handed on to us by those who from the beginning were eye-witnesses and servants of the word' (1:1–2). The Father and the Spirit would be witnesses, as it were, from a heavenly perspective. But the incarnation was an earthly event, and it needed earthly witnesses too. That was to be the responsibility of the apostles, and the faith of many millions of Christians down the succeeding centuries has been founded on the reliability of their testimony. With all their faults, these were manifestly honest men, and their unanimous evidence has provided the Christian Church with enormous confidence in proclaiming its message. These eleven were indeed eye-witnesses—of the miracles, of the teaching, of the cross and of the resurrection. To them was to be added in due course a man who did not share their authority as an eye-witness, Paul of Tarsus, but whose credentials as an apostle were based on his Damascus Road experience and on a direct commissioning by the Holy Spirit, recognized and affirmed by the other apostles. Strangely, to modern thinking, Mary Magdalene was never cited in the early Church as a primary witness, on a par with the Eleven, despite the unanimous testimony of the Gospels to the fact that she was the first living person to see the risen Christ. She was an eye-witness, without doubt, but not an apostle.

However, all of this would have been impossible without the promise of the Spirit of truth. The disciples themselves must have been deeply aware of that. This tiny band, joined by a few score of other men and women who had followed Jesus from Galilee or been won to his cause during the Judean ministry, must have felt that the unbelieving and hostile world around them was impervious to their message. After all, it had rejected Jesus himself, miraculous works and all. Why should it listen to them? The only answer offered was, in the event, the only answer needed—the Advocate, the Spirit of truth. As Jesus was soon to unfold to them, 'the one who is in you is greater than the one who is in the world' (1 John 4:4).

Convincing a sceptical generation of the truth of the gospel is a daunting responsibility, but it is one that the Church has to accept. In what ways could these three 'witnesses'—the Father's word, the Son's mighty acts and the eye-witness evidence of the apostles—be used more effectively in proclaiming our message? And what role would the Advocate, the 'Spirit of truth', need to have in that?

21

A PARTING GIFT

'I have said these things to you to keep you from stumbling. They will put you out of the synagogues. Indeed, an hour is coming when those who kill you will think that by doing so they are offering worship to God. And they will do this because they have not known the Father or me. But I have said these things to you so that when their hour comes you may remember that I told you about them. I did not say these things to you from the beginning, because I was with you. But now I am going to him who sent me; yet none of you asks me, "Where are you going?" But because I have said these things to you, sorrow has filled your hearts. Nevertheless I tell you the truth: it is to your advantage that I go away, for if I do not go away, the Advocate will not come to you; but if I go, I will send him to you.'

JOHN 16:1–7

This closing part of the discourse seems to have had two main objectives. The first was to make the warning very clear that what lay ahead for the followers of Jesus was to be far from a bed of roses. The second, mentioned here almost in the same breath, is that he was telling them these things now so that when the events eventually happened the disciples would remember, and see that it was all within the ultimate purpose of God.

He had already told them this twice, and there would be four more repetitions before the evening was over. Clearly this was important to Jesus. He didn't want the disciples to think that they had somehow fallen outside the will of God simply because opposition and persecution came to them.

The particular opposition mentioned here is excommunication from the synagogue, an experience that was to become a familiar one to Christians over the next century as the rift between Judaism and its messianic offspring became wider and more bitter. However, we have already read in this Gospel of a blind man healed by Jesus being threatened with this fate (9:22). There is little doubt that the actual expression used here refers to the later experiences of the Church at the time when the Gospel was being written, but it was not long after Pentecost before the first disciples began to experience the wrath of the religious authorities: the stoning of Stephen is a vivid example (Acts 7).

It is a sad commentary on religious fanaticism, in all its manifestations, that not only the Jews of the first two centuries but many Christians—and Muslims, too—throughout subsequent history have genuinely believed that they were 'offering worship' to God by persecuting those they regarded as heretics. Even where a veneer of civilization inhibits physical torture or cruelty, there can be few harsher tongues and few more virulent critics than a religious bigot in full spate. Twelve years editing a Christian monthly and twenty years in the BBC religious broadcasting department taught me that politicians get off lightly by comparison!

The disciples are not to allow this to cause them to 'stumble' —the word is literally to be 'scandalized'. The phrase can also imply 'giving offence', but the context here suggests that what Jesus was concerned about was the possibility that under this kind of pressure his chosen followers might 'fall down' and fail. So the assurance that this persecution was part of the divine picture was important. What would happen to them would not be an accident or a failure on God's part to protect his own. Bluntly, this was simply how it was going to be, but the rewards would be great—above all, the reward of knowing oneself to be within the Father's will, just as the Son was, despite what lay ahead for him.

So the point was made again, and reinforced: 'I did not say these things to you from the beginning, because I was with you.' That phrase 'from the beginning' is also something of a theme in the discourse, as though Jesus wants to emphasize on this particular occasion the reality of their personal experience of him, which is the ground of their apostleship.

Jesus then returned to the painful subject of his imminent departure: *'but now* I am going'... back to 'him who sent me', the Father. Earlier they had asked him where he was going (14:5), yet now they were silent. Sorrow had filled their hearts, curiosity replaced by anxiety. Jesus gently rebuked them. There was no real ground for sorrow or anxiety, because his departure would in the long term be to their advantage, however difficult it was for them to believe it at that moment. If Jesus were *not* to go away, the promised Helper would not come, the one Jesus would send from his Father.

In any case, as they must surely have realized, Jesus would have to go sooner or later, in fulfilment of God's greater purpose. And part of that greater purpose was the coming of the Holy Spirit, the Spirit of truth, the Helper and Advocate who they had been promised would be theirs. Even if they could not, in their humanity, be glad that their teacher was leaving them, surely they could appreciate the generosity of the gift, and share in the joy of Jesus that his task on earth was nearly completed—that for him it was time to go home?

The truth is that we always find it hard to see beyond the present, because we are time-bound creatures. As a child, I could never appreciate the promise of 'jam tomorrow'. It may seem pointless to a teenager to prepare at fourteen for exams that won't take place for two years or more. Even as an adult, it is sometimes hard to see the value of investing in a pension, for instance, when the money could be spent and enjoyed now. Try as we may, we are children of the moment, and in that, at least, we can understand how the disciples felt. Nevertheless, when the reward finally comes—the birthday party for the child, the exam results for the teenager, the pension for the person facing retirement—we can see the truth of what we were told long before.

It would be so for the disciples, of course, in just a few weeks' time. But in that upper room, with darkness outside and a sense of foreboding filling their hearts, it was understandably hard for them to appreciate the glory that lay ahead.

'Do not store up for yourselves treasures on earth, where moth and rust consume and where thieves break in and steal; but store up for yourselves treasures in heaven' (Matthew 6:19–20). It is a theme of the teaching of Jesus that short-term goals are fleeting and that his followers should aim for the more lasting ones. In what ways can we lift our sight day by day above the pressing present, to 'store up treasures in heaven'?

22

CONVICTED OF SIN

'And when he comes, he will prove the world wrong about sin and righteousness and judgment: about sin, because they do not believe in me; about righteousness, because I am going to the Father and you will see me no longer; about judgment, because the ruler of this world has been condemned.'

JOHN 16:8–11

Now Jesus explained to them what the work of the Advocate-Helper would be in relation to the 'world'. For them, and for those who would follow them as his disciples, the Spirit would be a Helper and one who would support their cause, arguing their case like an advocate in court. But for the world—society organized as though God did not exist—his role would be a quite different one.

He is still the 'Advocate' and the language is still that of legal justice, but now he is not the lawyer for the defence but for the prosecution. Briefed by God, as it were, he will argue the case against the unbelieving, Christ-rejecting world—indeed, he will go beyond mere argument, he will 'prove' or 'convict' them of their sin. Like prosecuting counsel, he will build a case against them, and this case will find them guilty on three counts. They have been wrong about sin, wrong about righteousness, and wrong about judgment.

Just as the Greeks had several words for 'love', so they had several for 'sin'. The one used here, *hamartia*, carries the sense of failure to reach a required standard, 'falling short'. This failure was pre-eminently failure to recognize and believe in the one God had sent: 'because they do not believe in me'. That is not just a matter of theological understanding, as though they were to be penalized for incomprehension or ignorance, but of wilful refusal to believe. This judgment has already been explained earlier in the Gospel: 'This is the judgment, that light has come into the world, and people loved darkness rather than light because their deeds were evil' (3:19). In other words, there was an element of moral choice involved.

Of course, there still is and always will be a choice. Many times I have sat with someone, arguing the case for faith in Christ, only to be met with one intellectual objection after another. As each objection was dealt with, another would be found—but in the end, very often, the issue was revealed in quite different terms: 'If I were to believe in him, I'd have to change my life... and I don't want to.' Underneath many an apparently rational or cultural objection to Christianity there lurks a moral issue, and that is the real sticking point. The sin of those who saw and heard Jesus but refused to believe in him was, at heart, a moral one, and it was that sin, not some excusable failure to understand, of which they were to be found guilty.

In what way, then, would the Spirit prove the world wrong about 'righteousness'? To answer that involves looking rather more carefully at the word 'righteousness', which is not a common one in this Gospel. In fact, this is the only time the Gospel uses this particular Greek word, though it is one much loved by Paul, who uses it no less than 32 times in his letter to the Romans.

It means 'doing what God requires'—in other words, 'justice'. The world was to see Jesus executed as a criminal, having judged him to be an impostor and a rebel against God. But through the cross and resurrection, the Spirit will now do two things: demonstrate that Jesus was 'right' all along ('doing what God required') and that God is scrupulously 'right' and just in his dealings.

Finally, the Spirit will 'prove the world wrong' about judgment. The world will see Jesus judged before the Sanhedrin and the Roman governor, and led out to death. But that will not be the true judgment, literally the 'critical moment' (the word for 'judgment' is *krisis*). The real judgment will be that of the 'ruler of this world', who will stand condemned when Jesus is vindicated by God at the resurrection.

So 'the world' is wrong on all three counts, and it will be part of the work of the Spirit to 'prove' it, to press home the case. It still is. Only the Spirit of truth can finally convince people of these truths. As Paul said, they are 'discerned spiritually'. They are 'not taught by human wisdom but taught by the Spirit' (1 Corinthians 2:13–14). Sometimes, when we are struggling to convince a friend or colleague of the truths that have changed our own lives, or are struggling ourselves with some aspect of the faith, we need more than anything else to call to our aid the Holy Spirit, the Spirit of truth. No one yet, I'm convinced, was ever 'argued into the kingdom' by anything less. This should also teach us a proper humility about truth. It isn't *our* truth, but God's, and his Spirit may wish to teach us lessons from unexpected sources.

The world is wrong about many things in the spiritual realm, but only the Spirit of truth can convince people of error. In what ways do Christian preachers and evangelists, and all who set out to bear witness to the good news, need to bear that in mind and let it shape their approach? How can the 'Spirit of truth' deliver us from religious arrogance?

23

THE SPIRIT OF TRUTH

'I still have many things to say to you, but you cannot bear them now. When the Spirit of truth comes, he will guide you into all the truth; for he will not speak on his own, but will speak whatever he hears, and he will declare to you the things that are to come. He will glorify me, because he will take what is mine and declare it to you. All that the Father has is mine. For this reason I said that he will take what is mine and declare it to you. A little while, and you will no longer see me, and again a little while, and you will see me.'

JOHN 16:12–16

People sometimes, and not unreasonably, ask how we can be so sure that what was remembered of the teaching of Jesus was close to what he actually said. They sometimes cite the party game of 'Chinese Whispers', where a message whispered into the ear of one person and then passed on in whispers around the whole group emerges extremely distorted and often ludicrously wrong at the other end. They fear that something like that has happened to the teaching of Jesus in the New Testament. After all, they say, it was a long while after the event that the Gospels were written— plenty of time for the 'Chinese Whispers' to do their work.

Their anxiety can be answered in two ways, it seems to me. At the purely practical level, the message of Jesus wasn't passed on in whispers. His words were regarded as too important for that. On the contrary, they were cherished, learnt by heart, recited aloud in groups of Christians in the various churches around the Middle East, until the time, thirty or forty years after his death, when they were finally recorded in writing in the books we know as the Gospels. This 'oral record', as it is called, has been shown to be extremely reliable when used in this way, especially by people who *had* to use their memories all the time because they could neither read nor write. That's one answer, and it is backed up by a great deal of research and evidence.

The second answer is the spiritual one, and it is given here by Jesus. It would be a specific work of the Holy Spirit to 'guide' the apostles into 'all the truth'. Later, as we shall see, he was to make that promise even more specific in relation to his own teaching. After all, what would be the divine purpose in a faulty or misleading account of the teaching of Jesus? If his words were 'life', as he claimed, then it seems very important that their life-giving truth should be handed on to all those who would come to believe in him.

Certainly the early Church saw itself as the repository of a veritable treasure of truth which came from Jesus—what it called 'the tradition'—and it recognized a solemn responsibility to pass this 'deposit' on to future generations. So the promise of Jesus that the Holy Spirit would guide his followers into 'all the truth' was seen as central to their ministry.

Of course, we need to set limits on the interpretation of these words. Some people have claimed, and still do, that this means the Church (however we define it) cannot ever be wrong about anything, because it is guided by the Holy Spirit. He is there to guide the Church, not to be used by it. This is true of great decisions and small ones—in PCCs, deacons' meetings and so on. It's not unknown for someone to suggest that as the Spirit's guidance has been asked for in the deliberations, then whatever has been decided must be God's will, whether it's green paint for the vestry walls, a new clock for the tower or the choice of a new vicar. No such *carte blanche* is proposed here! Neither should this be pushed into extravagant claims about the Bible's authority. Its truth is profound, and needs wise and humble quarrying.

'The truth' is a very particular concept in John's Gospel. Jesus is 'the truth' (14:6). God's word is 'truth' (17:17). The purpose of God is 'truth' (18:37). Those who wish to know the truth, or do the truth, or practise truth, must 'come to the light' (of Christ) (3:21). As with prayer, truth is sought and found 'in his name', and *only* in his name.

So 'all the truth' is actually 'truth in its fullness', the truth of God—truth revealed in his Son. What Jesus promised the disciples here in the upper room was that the Holy Spirit would continue that work of revelation in them, including truths that would perhaps be too painful, or completely beyond their comprehension, at this stage of their own discipleship. This is, as Richard Burridge says, a promise of 'life-long learning'.

By this process the Holy Spirit would 'glorify' Jesus, by taking what was 'his' (his message, his work, and everything the Father had sent him to do) and declaring it to them. Jesus was careful to avoid any suggestion that this glorification would somehow detract from the glory of the Father. 'All that the Father has is mine. *For this reason* I said that he will take what is mine and declare it to you'. There is no division in the Godhead. Father, Son and Spirit work in perfect harmony towards the same goal. God's word is truth. Jesus is the truth. And the Spirit is the 'Spirit of truth'.

The last teasing sentence about Jesus soon being beyond his disciples' sight and then 'in a little while' within their sight again apparently changed the subject. In fact, it was a bridge into the last section of his discourse, as we shall see.

What ought it to mean for the individual Christian, and for the Church, that the Holy Spirit is the source of 'truth in its fullness', as Jesus said? How should we handle issues of truth in our own lives? And what claim can the Church justifiably make to be the 'pillar and bulwark of the truth' (1 Timothy 3:15)? In practice, how might we expect the promise to be fulfilled that the Holy Spirit will 'lead us into all the truth'?

24

AFTER A LITTLE WHILE

Then some of his disciples said to one another, 'What does he mean by saying to us, "A little while, and you will no longer see me, and again a little while, and you will see me"; and "Because I am going to the Father"?' They said, 'What does he mean by this "a little while"? We do not know what he is talking about.' Jesus knew that they wanted to ask him, so he said to them, 'Are you discussing among yourselves what I meant when I said, "A little while, and you will no longer see me, and again a little while, and you will see me"? Very truly, I tell you, you will weep and mourn, but the world will rejoice; you will have pain, but your pain will turn into joy.'

JOHN 16:17–20

If, as we have already speculated, the disciples were now out-doors, perhaps strolling through the temple courts, it would certainly provide a suitable setting for this little scene. Jesus had said several times that 'in a little while' he would be leaving them to go to the Father: the Greek word is *mikron*—in 'micro-time', we might say. Now, however, he added a complication to the forecast. In another *mikron*, 'in a little while', they would see him again. So they *wouldn't* see him, and then they *would* see him. It was all too baffling. Perhaps some straggled behind him, or deliberately slowed down, to ask each other—out of earshot of the Master, as they thought—'What's he talking about? We haven't got a clue!'

Their bafflement was understandable, and complicated by all the talk of the Helper, the Advocate, who would come to their aid after his departure. Did Jesus mean that he was going to die? That was really too terrible to contemplate. Did he mean he would somehow be caught up to God, like Elijah of old? Did he mean that this 'Spirit of truth', to be sent to them by him, was a substitute for his presence, or an addition to it? It's necessary to reflect that they must have been under great emotional strain, given the circumstances in which they found themselves.

It's also likely that the question they asked, which John makes rather a lot of here, was one that, in a slightly different context, was being asked constantly in the early Church for whom this Gospel was written. For the Christians of the second century, the 'second coming' of Jesus was to become something of a tortuous issue, well summarized in the question put into the mouth of 'scoffers' by the author of the second letter of Peter: 'Where is the promise of his coming?' (2 Peter 3:4). It was all very well Jesus promising that they would 'see him again', but *when*?

In fact, the promise that Jesus made here to the disciples, in context, referred simply to his death and resurrection. In a 'little while', after his arrest, trial and crucifixion, they would not 'see' him: the word used here means more than simply to see with the eyes, but carries the implication of 'beholding', of watching with interest and attention. From that moment he would not be there for them to 'see' and have him as a model and exemplar. Then again, after a little while, they *would* 'see' him (the verb is now the ordinary one for vision), when he stood before them as the risen Lord. The great claim of the apostles, of course, was this: 'We have seen the Lord.'

So, while there would be a difference, it would all be contained within the single great 'event', Christ's 'glorification', the saving action of God through his Son in his death and resurrection. This seems to be underlined in the words of Jesus as he overheard their questions and tried to put their minds at rest.

'Very truly [amen, amen], I tell you, you will weep and mourn, but the world will rejoice; you will have pain, but your pain will turn into joy.'

Here was the clearest indication he had given them that his 'going away' involved death—'weeping and mourning' are the words used to describe what happened at a funeral (see, for example, 11:33). They would be cast down in despair and grief, but it would only be temporary, for a 'micro-time'. Then their pain would turn into joy, as their eyes saw him again—in the very room they had just left, and in Galilee. It is true that, in the longer perspective, Jesus also promised that 'every eye' would one day behold him, risen, ascended and glorified (Revelation 1:7), but on that day, while the Christians might justifiably 'rejoice', the nations of the earth—the unbelieving world—would 'wail' at their failure to recognize him.

But that was in the long view, not the 'little while', not the 'micro-time' that Jesus now held before his anxious followers. Perhaps they shrugged their shoulders at this point, and simply resumed their evening walk, still baffled, but hoping that light would dawn. Perhaps they began to glimpse the greater truth that the 'beloved disciple' came to see clearly in later days. For the last few minutes of his discourse, Jesus bent his efforts to that end.

As century follows century of the Christian era, and indeed millennium follows millennium, it is remarkable that the resurrection of Jesus is still the determining truth of Christianity. It still turns sorrow to joy, despair to hope. But does that 'longer perspective' mean as much to us today—that Christ will come again, to be seen and worshipped on earth?

25

The moment of joy

'When a woman is in labour, she has pain, because her hour has come. But when her child is born, she no longer remembers the anguish because of the joy of having brought a human being into the world. So you have pain now; but I will see you again, and your hearts will rejoice, and no one will take your joy from you. On that day you will ask nothing of me. Very truly, I tell you, if you ask anything of the Father in my name, he will give it to you. Until now you have not asked for anything in my name. Ask and you will receive, so that your joy may be complete.'

JOHN 16:21–24

It would seem that there weren't any of the women disciples present in the upper room on that night. This is slightly surprising, as Luke tells us quite specifically that they *were* there after the ascension (Acts 1:13–14). But it seems unlikely that Jesus would have used this illustration of a woman in labour if there had been women present who had rather more personal experience of it than he had.

It is a very vivid picture, probably more vivid to people in the first century, when birth was not assisted by analgesics—or even exercises learnt at ante-natal classes! The rate of perinatal mortality until the modern era always made childbirth a dangerous and painful business, yet of course without it the human race would have ceased to exist. Such is the urge to procreate, and such, specifically, the maternal instinct, that the joy of the ultimate goal—a child—has always been deemed sufficient incentive. Incidentally, whatever the old translations may say, her joy was not about the birth of a boy rather than a girl. The word used, *anthropos*, is the one for a human being of either gender.

The point about the hour of childbirth was well made in context. Jesus' 'hour had come'. He had said so. He had also indicated that it would be a time of pain and anguish, the thought of which filled him with sorrow and the disciples with apprehension. But, he had assured them, it was only for a 'little while'—just like the hours of a woman's labour. It's impossible for a man to comment, in a way, but I suppose that the difference between labour pains and (say) the pain of an inoperable disease is that the one will soon end, and in joy, while the other may be terminal. Before the days of pain control or effective surgery, people were used to the idea of simply enduring pain, but it must have been easier to do so if one knew that there was a positive reward at the end of the suffering.

In much the same way, the disciples would sorrow and grieve, but there was an end to their sorrow, and it would be as rewarding as the birth of a child. Doubtless several of the disciples were parents, and could relate to the experience personally.

This joy, Jesus said, would be of an enduring quality rather than a temporary lift of the spirits: 'No one will take your joy from you.' Outward circumstances, even the implacable opposition of 'the prince of this world', would not be able to rob them of it: 'Your hearts will rejoice.' At that moment, this may have seemed far from their experience, which probably combined apprehension about the death of their master with fear about the long-term consequences of following him. They had clung to him, but rather like voyagers caught in a storm, holding on because, frankly, they could see no alternative. 'To whom *can* we go?' Peter had replied defiantly, when challenged by Jesus about their continuing commitment to him. 'You have the words of eternal life'—you, and presumably no one else (see John 6:67–68).

It is that very future to which Jesus now turns their attention. 'On that day'—the day when their hearts will rejoice—they would 'ask nothing of him'. Yet, he goes on at once to say, they were to 'ask in his name... so that their joy may be complete'. It sounds like a straightforward contradiction, or else a rebuke: you will ask nothing, but you *should* ask for anything, and receive it, for that 'joy' to be fulfilled.

In fact, Jesus used two different Greek words for 'ask'. In that day they would have *no more questions*: that is the implication of the word 'ask' in verse 23. Now they were full of them, as we have seen in the course of this one evening, but 'on that day' the questions would cease because they would have another Teacher who, as we have learnt already, would guide them into 'all the truth'. This should not be taken to imply that there is something wrong in asking questions, but as an assertion that the followers of Jesus would 'on that day' have access to a constant source of reassurance in the promised Advocate. Questions intended to elicit an answer are one thing; anxious doubts expressed as questions are another.

So, not for the first time, the disciples are urged to 'ask' the Father, in the name of Jesus, not for information, but for the things that will make for their peace—'so that your joy might be complete'.

One large question remains. What, or when, is 'that day'? Is it the 'Day of the Lord', the promised time when the Messiah will claim the kingdom and bring in God's perfect rule of justice and peace? Or is it rather the approaching 'day' of Christ's glorification, when the purpose of God in sending his Son would be fulfilled and his victory over the powers of evil demonstrated? Would it, perhaps, be found only in heaven, where the will of God is perfectly done?

Or is it, as the context might suggest, the day when the Spirit would come in power as the gift of the Father and the Son to the new community of God, the Church? I find this much the most satisfying explanation, mainly because it seems to spring from the text itself. Anyone hearing these words for the first time, or simply reading them in the Gospel, would assume that they referred to the coming of the promised Spirit, with all that that would mean for the bereft disciples. This, after all, would happen 'in a little while', hot on the heels of the resurrection, rather than at some undisclosed future date. Quite soon their questions would be answered; quite soon they would find that their prayers made 'in his name' would also be answered. And the consequence would be pure joy.

Can we distinguish between the kind of 'asking' that is an honest search for the truth and that which is much more the expression of anxious doubt? 'Not to know' is not a sin; honest doubt is not a sin; but there is something sinful, or at least spiritually demoralizing, about nourishing in our hearts and minds doubts and anxieties. As a wise man once said, 'You can't stop the birds flying overhead, but you can stop them making a nest in your hair'!

LIFE AND GLORY

26

'NOW WE CAN SEE'

'I have said these things to you in figures of speech. The hour is coming when I will no longer speak to you in figures, but will tell you plainly of the Father. On that day you will ask in my name. I do not say to you that I will ask the Father on your behalf; for the Father himself loves you, because you have loved me and have believed that I came from God. I came from the Father and have come into the world; again, I am leaving the world and am going to the Father.' His disciples said, 'Yes, now you are speaking plainly, not in any figure of speech! Now we know that you know all things, and do not need to have anyone question you; by this we believe that you came from God.'

JOHN 16:25–30

John's Gospel has no 'parables' in the sense that the others do—stories of field and farm, home and lake. But it does indeed have many 'figures of speech'—allegories, enigmatic sayings, extended metaphors. There have been the shepherd, the door of the fold, the travel lodge with its rooms, the vine and its gardener. Allegories are fine, but the problem lies in the interpretation! Several times already people have asked Jesus to speak 'plainly' (see, for example, 7:4; 10:24), and quite recently in this Gospel Jesus had finally resorted to what he called 'plain speech' to explain his rather enigmatic language about the death of Lazarus.

As the beloved disciple remembered the teaching of Jesus, it had this mystical and elusive quality about it. It would be wrong to suggest that the teacher described in the other Gospels always spoke 'plainly': his parables were, for most of those who heard them, not windows into understanding but puzzles only to be solved by those who had 'ears to hear'. But there is a unique visionary and allegorical element in the fourth Gospel, which is at the same time its deepest treasure and its greatest challenge.

But now, praise be, the Master was going to speak 'plainly' of the Father—no more vines and gardeners, no more mysterious 'Advocates', just the facts. But still they would have to wait: 'The hour is coming... On that day...' And when that time of enlightenment came, which we may assume means when the Spirit of truth was theirs, they would at last do what Jesus had many times urged them to do: 'Ask the Father in my name'. The difference would be that now they would no longer need Jesus alongside them as an intermediary. 'The Father himself loves you, because you have loved me and have believed that I came from God.' This didn't mean that they would no longer be praying 'in the name of Jesus', but that they would not be depending on his presence with them to guide and order their prayers.

There follows a sentence that must have shone for them like sunshine breaking through cloud. Certainly its meaning was crystal clear and unambiguous and its language as simple as anyone could want: 'I came from the Father and have come into the world; again, I am leaving the world and am going to the Father.' In 23 words, of a simplicity that a child could under- stand, the whole Christology of John's Gospel—how it sees the nature and work of Jesus—is summarized. What the prologue expressed in terms of 'the Word made flesh' (1:1–14) is here set out in 'plain speech'. This is how the beloved disciple wants us to understand the nature and meaning of Jesus: he came from God, he dwelt among us, and then he returned to God.

At any rate, the disciples, who had constantly struggled with the enigmatic side of Jesus' teaching, were enormously relieved. 'Yes,' they said, 'now you are speaking plainly, not in any figure of speech! Now we know that you know all things, and do not need to have anyone question you; by this we believe that you came from God.'

Their relief is plain to see, but their delight at it seems premature. Had they *really* taken on board the implications of what Jesus had been telling them? Were they listening properly when he spoke of the pain and anguish of childbirth that precedes the joy of parenthood? Had they forgotten the betrayal and death that lay ahead for their master? Jesus responded to their enthusiasm with what sounds like a dose of cold water. 'Do you *now* believe?' The repetition of the word 'now' in this whole passage creates a kind of motif, as does the constant emphasis on the word 'know'. He wanted them to know and he wanted them to believe, but he also wanted to be sure that they understood what they claimed to know and appreciated the challenge of what they professed to believe. 'The hour is coming, *indeed it has come*, when you will be scattered, each to his home, and you will leave me alone.' Did they *know* that? Did they believe his words?

Of course, it happened, and it would seem that the purpose of Jesus in issuing these warnings was so that when it did happen, their faith would be strengthened (16:4). If the promised time, 'the hour', had now come (or was about to come), then the moment of their testing was at hand. For all their protestations to the contrary, some of them would deny him and all of them desert him at his arrest. It would be then, in the moment of their ultimate trial, that they would need to remember and believe, clinging to his words through the anguish and pain and looking for the joy 'which no one can take from you'. It was then that they would need to believe that neither Jesus nor his followers were ever to be 'alone', because the Father who loved them would be with him, and consequently with them. The real test of their belief in him, in other words, would not take place in the upper room, but in the outer darkness.

Most of us have moments in life when we feel that what had previously been obscure has become crystal clear. Perhaps we can recollect them. Sometimes it has taken place because someone has explained something to us in words or language that we can readily understand. But then the real challenge remains: can I live by the truth that has now been revealed to me?

PERFECT PEACE

'I have said this to you, so that in me you may have peace. In the
world you face persecution. But take courage; I have conquered
the world!'

JOHN 16:33

They had sat there listening to him since supper, with just
an occasional interjection or anxious question. We can picture
them—young men, most of them rugged and tanned from
outdoor work in field or on the lake, unsophisticated Galileans
(regarded as yokels by the smart set in Jerusalem), gathered
around the equally young man who addressed them. He was
their sole point of reference, the source of whatever unity of
purpose they had. All of them, we may assume, were by now
committed at least to the firm conviction that he was the
Messiah, in itself a quantum leap of thinking for devout Jews
(which they were).

Some, of course, like Simon the Zealot, would have been
engaged in the struggle for the recovery of Israel's independ-
ence and sovereignty long before they met Jesus. For the
Zealots, the first-century equivalent of modern 'People's Revolutionary Movements', the only good Roman was a dead one,
and there would be no restoration of Israel until the last of
the invaders had left the land. What was it in the teaching or
personality of Jesus that attracted Simon to a man who advocated turning the other cheek and loving one's enemies?

But there was also Matthew the tax collector, called from the tax booth and the service of the hated conquerors to follow a man who advocated the virtues and blessings of poverty. What brought him to this place and this position?

The discourse was almost over, and perhaps Jesus, looking at them, felt for a moment the enormity of the task that he was leaving them to do. Of course, he had promised the divine Helper, the Advocate, to be with them and in them for ever. But that was not yet. And he had spoken of persecutions and tribulations that lay just ahead—'anguish and pain' were his words—out of which, it was true, would be born a deep and lasting joy. But the pain was imminent and the joy in the future. And to deepen their sense of anxiety, he had spoken repeatedly of his 'leaving' them, 'going to the Father'. For a group of disciples, there could be no worse fate than that the teacher should be removed and they be left to fend for themselves. Jesus had just warned them that they would be 'scattered': 'and you will leave me alone' (16:32). Indeed, Matthew 26:31 and Mark 14:27 record an even more stark warning, when Jesus cited words of the prophet Zechariah (13:7): 'I will strike the shepherd, and the sheep of the flock will be scattered.' And the disciples seemed to know it. They sensed that they would soon be on their own, facing a hostile world, a furious establishment and the armed might of the world's greatest imperial power. Reason enough, Jesus might have felt, for the anxiety and fear etched on those homely faces.

So the discourse ended not with warnings but with words of reassurance and peace. He had not, and still did not, dilute the challenge that lay ahead of them: 'In the world you face persecution.' But now he wanted them also to hear words of peace. He had already bequeathed peace to them as his parting gift (14:27). Now he set out the grounds of that peace: it is in him, because he has conquered the unbelieving world.

The contrast between the words used for 'persecution' and 'peace' is instructive. 'Persecution'—*thlipsis*—is literally a word that means 'pressure', and so by reference affliction, trial or distressing circumstances. It is something that human beings have always known, modern ones every bit as much as those in the ancient world. In fact, the 'pressures' of modern life—no time, no space, no contact with simplicity—make 'pressure' an everyday experience for most people.

And that pressure is generated by 'the world', the *cosmos*—society that has neither time nor space for God. Of course, the Christian believer would like to have such time and space, but, as Wordsworth put it, 'the world is too much with us'. It makes its own demands and, in our struggle to meet them, time, space and simplicity are often the prime casualties. So when Jesus told his followers that 'in the world they would have *pressure*' he was speaking not only to them at that moment, on the brink of their apostleship, but to all of us who have followed them down the centuries in the apostolic faith.

But in contrast, in Christ they—and we—were to have 'peace', *eirene*. The balance is very precise: in the world, pressure; in Christ, peace. As the great prayer that followed would set out very clearly, the disciples were called to live fully and generously *in* the world, but not to be part of the world's *systems*: 'in', but not 'of'. But that very engagement with the world, which is a Christian duty and responsibility, would inevitably create pressure. The antidote was to 'abide' in Christ, because in him, like a shelter in a storm or a strong arm to lean on when we flag, there would be 'peace', and that peace would be the result of his 'conquest' of the world, his defeat of its priorities and power on the cross and in the empty tomb. Sin and death are its allies, but he would take on both and leave them mortally wounded. 'I have *conquered* the world!' On that basis, these anxious young men could take courage.

Jesus did not, of course, address them in Greek, which was the *lingua franca* of the time but not the language of hearth and home for these fervent Jews. To them he would have spoken in Aramaic, a Hebrew dialect of which a few words are still preserved in the Gospels (*Abba, talitha cumi, amen*). As we saw earlier, in Hebrew and Aramaic the word for peace was *shalom*, still the normal greeting heard in markets, shops and streets in Israel. It does mean 'peace', in the accepted sense of 'absence of strife', but it means a great deal more—blessing, wholeness, a state of living in peace and unity with God, neighbour and oneself. It is a truly lovely word, and it is not difficult for the Christian to see that these qualities are to be found supremely in Jesus, who lived in perfect unity and peace with God, with the people around him and with himself.

'Pressure', or 'peace'? It's not a straight choice, of course, because Jesus promised both. In the world we shall have pressure, because it is the nature of things; but in Christ we shall have peace, because it is his gift.

It's not hard to list the ways in which the world 'pressures' us, but it might be useful to look at our own list and see how much is the world's fault and how much our own! As for peace in Christ, what might be the essential clues to experiencing it, based on what Jesus has told his disciples in this discourse?

28

THIS IS LIFE

After Jesus had spoken these words, he looked up to heaven and said, 'Father, the hour has come; glorify your Son so that the Son may glorify you, since you have given him authority over all people, to give eternal life to all whom you have given him. And this is eternal life, that they may know you, the only true God, and Jesus Christ whom you have sent.'

JOHN 17:1–3

The bell had struck several times, but this, as it were, was the final stroke. 'These words' are presumably everything that Jesus had said to them in the upper room and since they left it, and most specifically perhaps the last words spoken at the end of the discourse—words of reassurance that he had 'overcome the world'. Now that the 'hour', which had been held in prospect for some time, had arrived, Jesus prepared for it on his knees, but looking 'up to heaven'. That seems a good example for anyone about to face a moment of crisis.

His prayer, probably the most intimate and moving of all the occasions when we overhear him in communion with the Father, is for the disciples as he leaves them, for all those who will believe in him during the coming years, and for the world, that it may come to know the love of God. It seems unlikely that anyone who was present could have recalled with such clarity the precise words that were used, but the beloved disciple, drawing on his own closeness to the master, undoubtedly captures here the heart of the Saviour's intercession.

His first request was that the Father would 'glorify' the Son. He had told the Greeks who had wished to speak to him a day or two earlier that 'the hour has come' when the Son of Man would be 'glorified' (12:23–24). After Judas left the upper room, Jesus told the disciples that '*now* the Son of Man has been glorified' (13:31). Here, for a third time, the strange language of 'glorification' is set within the earthly dimension of time... or is it the heavenly one? 'Father, the hour has come.' It's as though all through the later chapters of John the writer has been striking the chimes of a clock, and now the final stroke summons midnight. *This is it.*

This was the hour when the glory of God would be revealed in all its wonder and depth. In the very first sentence of this prayer, Jesus prayed that he might be 'glorified'—but only, it must be noted, so that the Father would also be glorified. Such was their unity of mind and purpose that glory for the one would be glory for the other. As the prayer proceeds, we are drawn further and further into the mystery of the glory of God and of his Son.

This is often called the 'high priestly prayer'. That may seem strange, as the prayer never once mentions priesthood or what are usually reckoned to be priestly concerns—the worship of the Temple and the offering of sacrifices. Yet it is wonderfully appropriate in the context of a true understanding of priest-hood. A priest, in the dictionary sense of the word, is someone who represents God to the people and the people to God—a kind of bridge builder between this world and heaven. Indeed, the Latin word for high priest is *pontifex*, literally 'bridge-builder', which seems an appropriate title for anyone who truly follows Jesus, our great high priest.

Here, Christ at prayer exemplifies the fundamental priestly concerns, which are to bring God to people and to bring people to God. In his case, that involved establishing a new kind of relationship between human beings and their Creator. Of that relationship this handful of men around him were to be the first model. So his prayer is primarily for them, but also, as we shall see, looking far beyond the present, for all those men and women down the ages who would follow in their footsteps as disciples of Jesus.

The gift he has for them from the Father is 'eternal life', which he (or possibly his narrator and interpreter in a kind of parenthesis) now defines: 'And this is eternal life, that they may know you, the only true God, and Jesus Christ whom you have sent.'

We notice that it doesn't say that God and Jesus are the *way* to eternal life, but that they *are* eternal life. What they are, eternal life is; and what eternal life is, they are. Right from the opening prologue of the Gospel we have been told that Jesus is 'life': 'in him was life' ... 'the Son gives life' ... 'just as the Father has life in himself, so he has granted the Son also to have life in himself' ... 'I am the resurrection and the life' ... 'I am the way, the truth and the life'. This life which Jesus has 'in himself' is nothing less than the life of God, which in the picture-language of Genesis was once breathed into Adam's nostrils, 'and the man became a living being' (Genesis 2:7).

Now this life of God, which is eternal because God is eternal, is available to all those who 'know' the Father and 'know' Jesus Christ. It is important to grasp the full import of this claim, because it might be loosely read as suggesting that those who know *about* God and Christ, or who hold to certain truths concerning their nature, words or works, automatically have eternal life. In fact, the word for 'know' used here is not the one for understanding, but relationship—the difference between 'knowing' that Charles is Prince of Wales and 'knowing' him as a person. Those who are at home with French will be familiar with the difference between the verbs *savoir* and *connaître*, both correctly translated as 'to know', but the first meaning to have 'learnt' or to 'understand', and the second meaning to 'be familiar with'. The true believer does not depend on a set of facts or doctrines for salvation, but upon a relationship with God through Christ, nurtured by prayer, worship, sacrament and obedience.

We can only get to know someone if we give them time, attention and even, dare I say it, devotion. It is in those ways also that we can come to 'know' God and his Son, partially at first, perhaps, but with growing intimacy and understanding, until the day the apostle describes when we shall 'know fully, even as [we] have been fully known' (1 Corinthians 13:12).

Eternal life is not the *reward* for 'knowing' God and Christ, even in this true sense. Eternal life *is* knowing God and Christ. Once we 'know' them, we have eternal life. The tenses are all present: 'This *is* eternal life.'

The process by which we come to 'know' God and Jesus Christ is one that often puzzles people. In ordinary human relationships, how do we set about getting to know someone? What must we bring to the process? And what, in the end, are its rewards?

29

THE TRUE GLORY

'I glorified you on earth by finishing the work that you gave me to do. So now, Father, glorify me in your own presence with the glory that I had in your presence before the world existed.'

JOHN 17:4–5

'Glorify' is simply not a word we ever use in normal speech. We may apply the adjective 'glorious' to a few things—a beautiful sunset, perhaps, or an exquisite cover drive at cricket, or the pageantry of a State Opening of Parliament. But we don't speak of them as 'giving' glory, glorifying.

'Glory' is a word that the Hebrew scriptures apply only to God—'the glory of the Lord'. Indeed, they sometimes speak of this glory as a visible presence. At the dedication of the Temple by Solomon, 'the glory of the Lord filled the house of God' (2 Chronicles 5:14), to the extent that the priests could not stand to minister.

In the Gospels, the 'glory of the Lord' shone around the Christmas angels and the frightened shepherds at the announcement of the birth of Jesus (Luke 2:9), and the disciples 'saw his glory' on the Mount of Transfiguration (Luke 9:32; John 1:14). Gradually in this way the language of glory was applied to Jesus as well as to the Father, as though he reflected on earth the glory of heaven. It was also recognized that, as the Messiah, he must at some time 'enter into his glory'. Indeed, the presumptuous sons of Zebedee sought the places on his right and his left hand 'in his glory' (Mark 10:37).

For John, this 'glory' is almost the defining quality of the Messiah. Early on, he says that the apostles 'have seen his glory, the glory as of the Father's only Son' (1:14). The first miracle—the water turned into wine at Cana—was said to have 'revealed his glory', so that 'his disciples believed in him' (2:11). If 'glory' is the distinguishing mark of God himself, then the Son shares his glory, and during his incarnation, step by step, as it were, that 'glory' is unveiled to human eyes.

What was this 'glory' of which Jesus prayed? Strangely, in one sense, it seems inescapable that it is his suffering and death. In that very significant incident with the Greek visitors to the feast, Jesus clearly identified his 'glorification' with the 'grain of wheat that falls into the ground and dies' (12:23–24). There might appear to be many paths to glory—the battlefield, the sports arena, the laurel wreath of the victor, indeed any example of victory and conquest. It would have seemed logical to ascribe 'glory' to the resurrection of Jesus, as the triumph of life over death. Yet the hour of Christ's glory, for him, was the hour when he was led bound and helpless to a cross, to become there the eternal symbol of sacrificial love.

That, we can assume, is the true key to glory. If 'God is love', as John tells us in his first letter (1 John 4:8), then God is revealed in acts of love, and never more gloriously (if we may use the word) than in an act of total, selfless and sacrificial love, like that shown on the cross. It might not have looked like 'glory' at the time, but glory was what it was. There is, as Jesus had recently reminded his disciples, no 'greater love' than that which willingly lays down life for another. That greater love was the 'work' which the Father had given him to do, and which he had now 'finished'—brought to completion. This is the language of the prophetic future, for there remained the small matter of an arrest, a trial, a scourging and a crucifixion, before a triumphant voice could cry, in a true past tense, 'It is *finished*!'

So this prayer, so intimate and precious, the beloved disciple's recollection of Jesus in communion with his Father on the night of his betrayal, begins with a request for glorification. Rightly, that is not where *our* prayers should start, mainly because we could never be as sure as he was that anything that brought glory to us would bring glory to the Father. Partly, that assurance was because of the dynamic unity of purpose that bound them in one mind; partly, as Jesus prayed here, because all that he did was done on his Father's authority. He is the source of eternal life for those who are his, but only because God has 'given him authority over all people'. It is in the exercise of that authority that its giver, the Father, would be glorified.

Jesus was not asking for a glory he had not already known, but for 'the glory that I had in your presence before the world existed'. This is a familiar theme of the fourth Gospel, though almost entirely absent from the other ones. By the time John wrote his lengthy memoir of the life, words, actions and meaning of his beloved master, there had been many years to reflect on the significance of this astonishing life. For him, there could be no other explanation of the nature of Jesus Christ than that he was divine—that he shared the divine nature from the beginning. So whereas Matthew's Gospel starts with Abraham, Luke's in the Temple and Mark's in the wilderness of Judea, John starts his in heaven 'in the beginning'.

This belief involves the concept of the 'pre-existence' of Christ—that his life did not begin in Mary's womb or in a stable in Bethlehem, but in the heavenlies, as the eternal Word, the expression of God. At a point in time, 'the Word became flesh and lived among us' (John 1:14). And then, a few years later, he returned to the Father, to resume the 'glory' that he had known 'since the foundation of the world'. That was what the Church had come to believe about Christ—not, as some people seem to suggest, after a long period of time, but almost as soon as the first Christians had had time to consider the implications of what Jesus said and did.

Paul records for us a beautiful hymn of the early Church, in which the mystery of the divine humiliation is set out in graphic steps. Jesus 'emptied himself' of the glory of heaven, 'taking the form of a slave', being born in human likeness, humbling himself and becoming 'obedient to the point of death, even death on the cross'. But, the hymn proclaims, 'therefore God also highly exalted him', conferring the name above all other names on his Son and ordaining that the whole of heaven as well as the whole of earth should offer him its praise and worship (see Philippians 2:5–11).

This passage in Paul's letter gives the lie to the notion that the pre-existence of Christ was a late invention of the Christian Church, because Philippians was written before the synoptic Gospels (Matthew, Mark and Luke) and long before John. It tells us that within thirty years of the death and resurrection of Jesus, the first generation of Christians were clear that he was the divine Son of God who had existed from the beginning and who now, after the resurrection, had returned to the glory of heaven.

Here, in this high priestly prayer, Jesus prayed for that which his Father had willed—that, the work on earth completed, he should return 'glorified' to the Father's side, not more glorious than before, but with a different quality of glory, that of One who had triumphed over God's greatest adversaries, sin and death. And in the glory of the Son, the Father—who had ordained the whole process from the beginning—would also be 'glorified'.

Although we would, rightly, be reluctant to pray for our own glorification, it is encouraging to think that whenever we complete a work that God has given us to do, there is 'glory'. A prayer attributed to Francis Drake recognizes this: 'It is not the beginning of the work, but the continuing of the same until it be thoroughly finished, that yieldeth the true glory.'

30

AND THEY BELIEVED

'I have made your name known to those whom you gave me from the world. They were yours, and you gave them to me, and they have kept your word. Now they know that everything you have given me is from you; for the words that you gave to me I have given to them, and they have received them and know in truth that I came from you; and they have believed that you sent me. I am asking on their behalf; I am not asking on behalf of the world, but on behalf of those whom you gave me, because they are yours.'

JOHN 17:6–9

The prayer shifts at this point from the glory of the Son to the needs of his followers. Jesus might have completed 'the work which you gave me to do', but the work of these disciples still lay in the future. A handful of men and women would become the agents in the unbelieving and largely hostile world of the message and works of love that Jesus had revealed to them. It really was a staggering task, and it is not surprising that the first subjects of his 'parting prayer' were this little band 'whom you gave me'.

Jesus recognized that the disciples, like all who turn to Christ, are God's 'gift', because 'no one can come to me unless drawn by the Father who sent me' (John 6:44). They *were* God's and they *became* Christ's by the will of the Father. We might note at this point that before choosing them Jesus spent the night in prayer to God (Luke 6:12). These were chosen people

—not, incidentally, 'men' in the gender sense but *anthropois*, people, to whom Jesus had 'made [God's] name known'. Literally, he had 'manifested' the divine name to them—shown them the very nature of God himself.

Jesus had more than once hinted at this through his use of the phrase 'I am', and most specifically in his use of the divine name in the statement, 'Before Abraham was, I am' (8:58)—a claim that led to the crowd stoning him for his 'blasphemy'.

In Jewish thought, and indeed generally in the ancient world, there was an almost mystic property to a name. Your name conveyed more than simply your identity: it expressed not just who you were but what you were in nature and character. So God's name was holy and sacred. Jesus had instructed his followers to make the first petition of their pattern prayer 'Hallowed be your name'—may your name be held in reverence. We may say 'What's in a name?' and Shakespeare may argue that a 'rose by any other name would smell as sweet', but the biblical writers would not have agreed. In revealing the name of God to his disciples, Jesus had shared with them the greatest secret there is—the nature and character of the Creator.

We may well ask how he had done this. Was it through his works of power, revealing a God of signs and wonders? Or was it (uniquely, we may feel) in revealing a largely hidden aspect of his character—his grace and love?

The Hebrew scriptures revealed many instances of God's power, not least in the creation itself, or in the parting of the Red Sea, or in the mighty deeds of Moses, Joshua and David. What we did not learn until the Incarnation was the overwhelming love that the Creator had for his creatures—that the one who made us loves us. 'God so loved the world'—yes, the God-rejecting, Christ-abusing world 'that he gave his only Son, that whoever believes in him should not perish, but have eternal life' (3:16). Perhaps only a human life of total self-denial, utter obedience to the Father's will and final offering of himself on the cross could reveal the full extent of that love.

That was the supreme work of Jesus, the Word made flesh—the divine *Logos*, in the language of this Gospel. And this Word, *Logos*, had been revealed to the disciples and they had kept it like a treasure to be defended and valued. This is the divine explanation, the key to understanding the mystery of God—his love.

When John writes in his first letter the apparently simple words 'God is love' (4:16), he is in fact opening this particular treasure chest. This is not a statement that 'God loves' or even that God is 'loving', but that he is, in his very nature, love. As stone is hard and water is wet, so God is love. No one had ever revealed that astonishing and fundamental truth about the character of God as clearly and unambiguously as Jesus had done, and was yet to do on the cross. That was the 'Word' which God had given to the disciples through Jesus, and there has never been a more significant one.

The distinguishing mark of these disciples was that they had come to understand that God himself was the source of all that Jesus said and did. That was a huge leap of understanding, of course. It embodies a principle that will surface again in this Gospel, that there is a double process at work: the Father sent the Son and gave him authority; now the Son is to send his disciples and give them authority. But all the while, and in each case, the source of the authority and power is the Father.

Jesus in this prayer specifically referred to 'the words' that the Father had given him and he had now given to the disciples. We can distinguish these 'words' from 'the word' mentioned in verse 6 ('they have kept your word'). The 'word' is the *Logos*, that great revelation of God made in the incarnation of his Son—God's explanation, as it were, of his great purpose for Jesus and the world. The 'words'—a different Greek word, *rhemata*—are literally 'things spoken', verbal utterances, whereas the 'Word' was a person. This must refer to the teachings of Jesus, which they are to accept as the teachings of the Father. The disciples have received them, and will be the primary agents of their transmission through the mission of the Church to the whole world. Again, what a responsibility!

No wonder Jesus made them the first focus of his prayer, distinguishing them from 'the world', not because he didn't care about the world but because it was through these disciples that the world would be blessed.

Words are precious things that can heal or destroy, and spread truth or falsehood, love or hate. How can we, in our day, cherish 'the words' that Jesus passed on to his first followers? And in that process, how important is it to recognize that in some fundamental way the truth that they convey 'comes from God'?

PROTECTED BY THE NAME

'All mine are yours, and yours are mine; and I have been glorified in them. And now I am no longer in the world, but they are in the world, and I am coming to you. Holy Father, protect them in your name that you have given me, so that they may be one, as we are one. While I was with them, I protected them in your name that you have given me. I guarded them, and not one of them was lost except the one destined to be lost, so that the scripture might be fulfilled.'

JOHN 17:10–12

Jesus had said that he was asking, interceding, at this point not for the unbelieving world, but for the little band of believers whom he had gathered around him, of whom the eleven with him now in the darkness were the present representatives. He had described them as 'those you gave me', but now qualified that statement in two ways.

Firstly, while God had given them to him, they were also his: indeed, he had been 'glorified' in them—an idea which we shall look at more closely later. But in the unity of Father–Son it was pointless to try to differentiate between what belonged to one or to the other: 'all mine are yours, and yours are mine'. God gave them to Jesus, but they had become his not by ceasing to belong to the Father, but by entering into a new kind of relationship with both the Father and the Son.

Here is the beginning of the doctrine of the Trinity as

Christians have come to understand it—a mystical union of three Persons, Father, Son and Spirit, each of them at the same time distinct and yet one in purpose, truth and nature. Jesus had already told them that when the Spirit came, he, Jesus, would 'come to them', but linked it with a reminder that the Father was in him and he was in the Father (see 14:17–20). So in the coming of the Spirit, the Father and the Son would come to the disciples in a new way. Because Jesus was 'in' the Father and they were 'in' Jesus, the Spirit could work to draw them into a new experience of this Trinity of love and power.

That may all sound incredibly obscure and academic. But when we grasp the heart of this great truth, it is in fact a transforming experience. We talk of 'asking Jesus into our lives', and echo the words of the apostle with his astonishing claim that his life was 'in Christ' and that Christ lived 'in' him.

But in fact that relationship with Christ draws us inescapably into relationship with the whole of the Trinity, no less! To be in Christ is to be in God. That is why what seems like a cold doctrine is, in truth, a life-changing revelation. We don't believe in the Holy Trinity simply as something we assert week by week in the Creed, or to distinguish ourselves from groups such as Jehovah's Witnesses or Christadelphians, but as a truth that affects every aspect of our lives as Christians. Our Creator loves us and gave his Son for us. 'The Son of God', says Paul, 'loved *me* and gave himself for *me*' (Galatians 2:20). And the Holy Spirit is our constant helper, guide and comforter, the one who brings us closer to the Father and closer to the Son by his subtle work of prompting, persuading and confirming. We have a Trinity faith. That is not an embarrassment but a rich and glorious experience.

What this prayer also underlines is that the believer belongs to God and to Christ: 'they are mine'; 'they are yours'. Sometimes we are tempted to talk as though God and Christ belong to *us*—'my personal Saviour'; 'you are my God'. But while those ideas are true enough at one level, as we 'receive' the

Saviour and, like the psalmist, make our own personal commitment to the God who loves us and cares for us, they should not disguise the greater truth. We are creatures, and we belong to our Creator. Indeed, as Christians we are doubly 'owned'. We are his by creation ('It is he that made us, and we are his', Psalm 100:3), and we are his sons and daughters by grace: in John's language, through welcoming Christ we have won the power (literally, authority) to become his children (1:12).

In one of the marvellous cartoons by Nick Park, Wallace gives his pet dog, Grommit, a collar for a birthday present. 'There,' he says proudly, as he puts it on the dog. 'You look as though somebody *owns* you now!' In a strange way, we all like to feel we 'belong'—it's one of the great hidden benefits of church membership, in fact—and especially to belong to someone who cherishes and values us. Our belonging to God and Christ is like that, not a servile thing but a joyful relationship of dependence and love. As Jesus had told the disciples that very evening, 'I do not call you servants any longer, because the servant does not know what the master is doing; but I have called you friends' (15:15). That did not mean that he could not go on to urge them to 'keep his commandments', but that the basis of his command was not a call to duty but a call to belonging.

So Jesus prayed for those who belonged to him, that God would protect them in the future, when he would not be physically with them as their teacher and example. Over the previous three years or so he had himself protected them 'in your name that you have given me'—a rather tortuous phrase, which might be more easily rendered, 'I have protected in your name those whom you have given me'. The 'name' of God, as we have seen, speaks of his character and nature. To invoke his 'name' is to call to aid everything that God is in that character and nature—his power, his authority, his justice and his love. Jesus had protected them, as it were, with this divine umbrella. Now he asked the Father to assume the same responsibility towards them in the future as he had in the past. '*Holy* Father', he called him, rather unusually, perhaps because it was that aspect of God's nature which he knew his disciples needed most of all—holiness. Certainly this passage led quite naturally into the next, in which he prayed that they would be 'sanctified', made holy (17:17).

This divine protection would ensure their unity—unity with one another, and unity within the will of the Father and the Son. That is the heart of this part of the high priestly prayer, the incorporation of the disciples into the profound unity of purpose that distinguishes the Holy Trinity.

Somewhere in that idea lies the explanation of the otherwise baffling statement, 'And I have been glorified in them'. How could the disciples—how can we—'glorify' Jesus? The answer must lie in the same way as Jesus glorified his Father, by living a life of willing obedience to his commands, completing the work the Father had given him to do. In fact, the disciples' glorifying of Jesus still lay in the future, but it would always have its roots in their understanding of their relationship to him. They belonged to him. They were his. They would keep his commandments. They would complete the work that he had given them to do.

That, in a word, is what it means to 'belong' to God. And that is how Christ is 'glorified' in us.

What does it mean to belong to the Church, which the New Testament calls the 'body of Christ'? Does it just mean some kind of minimal attachment, with occasional or even regular attendance at worship? Or does it mean the kind of 'belonging' of which Jesus spoke in this prayer, a relationship rooted in dependence and love, as life-changing in its way as marriage, in which a man and a woman pledge themselves to 'belong' to each other?

32

IN THE WORLD, BUT NOT OF IT

'But now I am coming to you, and I speak these things in the world so that they may have my joy made complete in themselves. I have given them your word, and the world has hated them because they do not belong to the world, just as I do not belong to the world. I am not asking you to take them out of the world, but I ask you to protect them from the evil one. They do not belong to the world, just as I do not belong to the world.'

JOHN 17:13–16

The first two sentences of this part of the prayer seem to be full of paradoxes. Jesus prayed that the disciples should be filled with his 'joy'—*his* joy, we notice, not theirs. For them, sorrow lay ahead, and rejection: 'the world has hated them'. But in some strange way, the joy that marked the character of Jesus would become theirs. More than that, it would completely fill them, to overflowing. That's the implication of the very emphatic form of the word translated here by 'made complete'.

This joy would not be vulnerable to the hatred of 'the world'. The 'world' would indeed hate them, because they didn't belong to it, and a godless society hates those who do not subscribe to its own preferences and values. Again we must be clear: the 'world', in John's usage, is society organized as though God did not exist, the very society which down the centuries had consistently refused to acknowledge his stand-ards, and which now, with the coming of the Messiah, had wilfully refused to recognize him. 'The world', thus defined, is not 'everybody', but the kind of human society which is in rebellion against its Creator.

That kind of society cannot tolerate those who do not join the ranks of the rebels. It could not then, and it cannot now. This explains the quite irrational hatred and scorn that sincere faith and even transparent holiness often seem to evoke. Some, of course, are drawn by these qualities, recognizing something of the Creator in them. But for others their very presence is a constant irritant and provocation. Because of this, the disciples, who by their calling and commitment could never belong to the rebel party, will be hated—a theme Jesus had already touched on (15:18–19).

This thought led Jesus on to a petition. He asked not that God would *remove* the disciples from the world, but that he would protect them *within* it. Herein lies a great truth, and a great tension for the Christian believer in every age. What does it mean to be 'in' the world but not to 'belong' to it? And how can we play our part in responding to this prayer?

The phrase that John uses, translated here as 'belong', is *ek tou* in Greek, literally 'out of' or 'from'. The disciples did not come 'out of' the world's womb: they were not the world's children, but Christ's. They therefore owed no allegiance to its false values and attitudes. But of course they lived 'in' the world, the *cosmos*, every bit as much as those who belonged to the rebel party that rejected the will of its Creator.

It is all a matter of allegiance, at heart. There are two possible allegiances for every human being—to the will and purpose of the Creator, or to the will and purpose of Evil. That may sound unhelpfully stark, and of course the division has many blurred edges, but nevertheless there is a wide gulf between those who acknowledge the reality and existence of God and respect his will, and those who consciously defy it, or live as though he didn't exist. Not all in the first group will be saints (far from it), and not all in the second group will be 'sinners', in the conventional sense. But to live apart from God is to create a secular world, and in a secular world there is no room for divine purpose, justice or love. The disciples, by their allegiance to Jesus, had cut themselves off from the secular world and its beliefs, but they still lived in the world God had created, the *cosmos*.

They followed the example of Jesus: 'They do not belong to the world, just as I do not belong to the world.' Jesus lived his earthly life knee-deep in the world and its concerns, but he never succumbed to its values. Indeed, they were the very temptations that he rejected in the wilderness—to use worldly means to attain spiritual ends. Now he prayed that the disciples would follow his example, totally immersed in the world's sorrows and joys, fully and completely human, but rejecting its rotten values and priorities.

They were not a set of plaster saints. They had squabbled, fought over who was the greatest, lost patience with the bewildered crowds thronging the Master. And ahead lay worse —Peter's betrayal, and the cowardly flight of the rest of them at his arrest. So Jesus was not praying for people who did not already know the insidious pull of worldly values. Even so, he did not pray that they should be completely removed from its influence—sent off to a hermitage, we might say. It was not going to be that 'easy'! They were to be in the world, in all its tawdriness, and they were to love it, as God did, and give themselves for it, as Christ did, but without identifying themselves with it.

That is a difficult equation, which has tested the Church all through its history. Sometimes Christians have felt that the only way to reject the world's values is to separate themselves completely from it. Thus some have felt it right to live for years on the top of poles in the desert, or in remote hermit caves. Mind you, they have often found that the world is not so easily avoided: it can infiltrate the imagination and will of the praying hermit as well as the compromising Christian in the casino.

It isn't simply a matter of deciding what is 'worldly' and what is 'spiritual' behaviour. Worldliness is an attitude of mind rather than a set of activities. The battle is an interior one, between the pull of the world and the pull of Christ. Many of us have taken great comfort from this prayer of Jesus, asking the Father to 'protect' us from 'the evil one' as we live out our lives in the world.

The word for 'protect' here is a very strong one, conveying the notion of being kept or guarded from harm. Jesus knew that his disciples—those there with him that night, and all the rest of us down the ages—would be called to live as witnesses to God's love in the world. He also knew the price and the risk of that calling, but it was unavoidable if that very world were to be brought back to the One who created and redeemed it. So he sought the greatest help that he could for his people in that mission—the powerful protection of the Father: 'I am not asking you to take them out of the world, but I ask you to protect them *from evil*' (NRSV footnote).

Sometimes the Church has become so like the world, in its desire to 'identify' with it, that it has been hard to see any difference between them. And sometimes the Church has been so 'heavenly minded' that it's been no use on earth! In practical ways, how can the paradox be resolved?

THE COMPLETION
OF THE TASK

33

MADE HOLY BY THE TRUTH

'Sanctify them in the truth; your word is truth. As you have sent me into the world, so I have sent them into the world. And for their sakes I sanctify myself, so that they also may be sanctified in truth.'

JOHN 17:17–19

For those who are reading this book through the days of Lent, we are approaching Palm Sunday, when we recall the arrival of Jesus and his Galilean followers in Jerusalem; the Master riding, not on a charger, as a conquering king might do, but on an ass, thus fulfilling the prophecy of Zechariah (9:9). His first port of call after that was the temple itself, where he proceeded to drive out the money changers and traders, thus 'cleansing' God's house. Only what was pure and clean could be used by the Lord—a principle that Jesus reflected on in this part of his high priestly prayer.

There are two key words here: 'sanctify' and 'truth'. Truth is a familiar idea, but modern people seldom, if ever, use the word 'sanctify'. It means, of course, to 'make holy', but the special sense here is of a person or thing being made holy for a purpose. The priests in the temple were 'sanctified' for their ministry: I suppose our word 'ordained' has something of the same meaning. In order to perform a holy function, they had to be set aside from secular activities, separated and made holy. But equally the sacrifices they offered—oxen, sheep or goats, mostly—had to be 'sanctified', set apart, regarded as peculiarly God's.

Here, Jesus spoke of both the disciples and himself being sanctified. He prayed that they might be 'sanctified in the truth' —a somewhat strange phrase, which presumably means that the 'truth' is what would make them holy and set them apart for their calling. Jesus then identified that truth: 'your word is truth'. This time he used *logos*, so we may assume he was referring to the whole revelation from God which they had received through Jesus, whom this Gospel has already called 'the Word' (1:1). That revelation was the truth—the truth about God, the truth about the world, the truth about themselves. It also truly revealed the way to God (14:6). We might think of this prayer as part of the 'ordination' of the apostles, their setting apart for a holy calling to be agents and ministers of that truth in the years after Jesus had left them.

But Jesus also said that he 'sanctified' himself. That is an interesting concept, because normally a person or an object was 'sanctified' by someone else, usually a priest. Moses 'sanctified' the people before Sinai, and then called on the priests to 'sanctify' themselves (Exodus 19:10, 22). Jesus, in saying that he sanctified himself, was performing a priestly function, a reminder that the Messiah was both king and priest. He set himself apart for the lonely but God-given task that lay ahead of him, and he asked his Father to set the disciples apart for the daunting responsibility that would be theirs in the coming days.

Jesus then set out the nature of that responsibility, which was their 'apostolate'. The Father had sent Jesus into the world as his agent; Jesus was now sending the disciples into the world as *his* agents. Just as Jesus was 'sent', so would they be 'sent': the verb provides the root of the word 'apostle'.

But it was not only the sending that was comparable, but its manner: '*as* you have sent me... so I have sent them'; in other words, *in the same way*. God sent Jesus as his representative and as evidence of his love for the human race. Jesus sent the disciples, and in fact sends his followers today, as his represent-atives and as evidences of his love for the world. It was a fearful responsibility for them, and it is a fearful responsibility for us.

It is true that the apostolic commissioning was at first re-stricted to this particular group of men and that that apostolic authority was uniquely theirs. But as we read the story of the emerging Church in Acts, we become aware that the apostolic responsibility was more widely shared—with 'certain women' (Acts 1:14), then with the so-called 'deacons' (Acts 6:3–8) and, of course, Paul of Tarsus (Acts 9:15). Later, the whole Church is called a 'royal priesthood', with the commission to 'proclaim the mighty acts of him who called you out of darkness into his marvellous light' (1 Peter 2:9).

So it would seem that this act of commissioning, so solemn and so central to God's purposes, embraces not only the Eleven gathered on this Passover evening, but, as we shall see, many, many other believers in Jesus in the future. Without being fanci-ful, we may feel that Jesus prayed for us on this holy evening, too—that we might be 'sanctified in truth' and 'sent... into the world'.

Here Jesus gathered into one sacred action his own calling and that of his people. All must be sanctified if their words and works are truly to be of God. Even the Son of God needed to sanctify himself for his calling. How much more should we, all too conscious of our human failings, weaknesses and sins, set ourselves aside for whatever part of God's mission in the world is our calling? For some it will be what we call 'the ministry' in its various forms. We all recognize that people need to be set apart and 'sanctified' for that. But for others it may be the Sunday school or youth group, the home meeting or lunches for older people, the witness to Christ's truth in business, factory, school or hospital... or the loving service of caring for family, friend or neighbour. It may be the struggle for justice for the oppressed, or the relief of suffering or poverty. The mission is all-embracing, because the world's needs are so diverse.

And it is 'into the world' that we have been sent—the very 'world' that John sees as Christ-rejecting, the world that will 'hate' his disciples for what they believe and teach. Yet it is also the very world that God loved so much, or in such a way, that he gave his only Son for its salvation.

Where is my own personal 'apostolate' to be exercised? How do I respond to the call to follow Christ's example and carry the love of God into a suspicious and sometimes hostile world? And what would it mean for me to 'sanctify' myself for this task?

THAT THEY MAY BE ONE

'I ask not only on behalf of these, but also on behalf of those who will believe in me through their word, that they may all be one. As you, Father, are in me and I am in you, may they also be in us, so that the world may believe that you have sent me.'

JOHN 17:20–21

At this point, Jesus broadened the scope of his prayer for the disciples to include all of those who would believe in him through their testimony—in other words, every Christian who has ever lived. Each of us may feel that we are included in this intercession, as all of us are part of the rich harvest of that apostolic message. As we do, we need to recognize its significance, for this is a prayer for Christian unity.

These verses have been taken up over the last century or so as a kind of watchword for the ecumenical movement. Christians and denominations of Christians should commit themselves to visible unity 'so that the world may believe'. Certainly these words of Jesus address the problem of Christian division and the blessing of Christian unity, but the particular situation of 'denominations' is strictly a modern phenomenon and only by extension could this petition of Jesus be applied to issues such as unity between Anglicans and Methodists, or Baptists and Lutherans.

Jesus knew the fragile nature of human fellowship. Already the tiny group of twelve had shown signs of falling apart—over their relative ranking in the team, over who would have the best seats at the kingdom banquet. Of course, most recently and grievously, there had been the defection of the betrayer, Judas. As the young Church began to grow after Pentecost, another set of divisions reared its head, most notably over the place of Gentiles in the Church, and later over the issue of Jewish food rules and rituals.

By the end of the third century, many more issues could be added to that list: the baptism of babies; the re-admission to communion of those who had compromised during the various persecutions; the extent to which charismatic practices should be welcomed in the Church; and also the emergence of various doctrines and interpretations of the faith, especially of the nature of Jesus Christ, which threatened orthodox Christian beliefs.

One of the clarion calls of some of the greatest of the early Church Fathers was to hold firm to the faith and not to divide the Church, because they could see that a divided Church would never be able to resist the mounting hostility of the world around them. It may well be that their anxiety led them sometimes to overstate the case, or to deal too harshly with what seem to us like minor deviations from orthodoxy. But it is all very well for us to be wise long after the event. As the spiritual battle raged for the survival of the Christian faith, they felt that there was no room for compromise and that unity of belief and behaviour was essential to that survival—and who, nearly two thousand years later, can argue with that?

It is against that kind of background that we should read these words of Jesus. As the beloved disciple recalled this moment of prayer perhaps as much as fifty years later, he was able to see it in that longer perspective. For him, the issue of disunity threatened the very survival of the Church. If Jesus had prayed that his disciples should be 'one', then let the Church hear and heed that petition as it entered the second century of its history. Indeed, he must have felt that if the prayer was not answered, then there was no hope for the Church's future.

Unity was not a luxury but an essential element in survival and future effectiveness in mission.

In fact, the prayer of Jesus sets the unity of his followers in a context far above and beyond church politics or organization. They are to be one, he says, 'as you, Father, are in me and I am in you'. The unity of the Church is to be built on the very principle that unites the Father to the Son, and that, as we have seen, is total, single-minded unity of will and purpose. At the beginning of his ministry, in the desert of Judea, Jesus had fought off the tempter's suggestions that he might go about his mission in his own way. To each temptation his reply was, in effect, the same: 'No, it is contrary to the will of God' (see, for instance, Matthew 4:1–11). At no point, not even in the face of the ultimate test in Gethsemane, did he waver from his fundamental allegiance: 'Yet, not my will but yours be done' (Luke 22:42). Nothing could divide his will, his purpose, from that of his Father.

That was the kind and quality of unity that Jesus prayed for his followers—not only the Eleven, not only the 120 disciples in the same room after Easter, but all who have believed in him down the centuries. He longed for a single-minded unity of will and purpose among his people. That might, or might not, mean the end of what we have come to call 'denominations'. I suspect that would be a secondary matter. The primary issue would be that visible and attractive unity of mind and purpose which alone would convince an unbelieving world that a 'new thing' was coming into being. Its purpose was so precise: 'that the world may believe that you have sent me'. Squabbling, dissenting Christians, whether in a local congregation or rival churches, is a denial of that unity of purpose and a crippling handicap to that mission. The world is all too familiar with splits, dissensions, squabbles and discord: they are the stuff of politics, of business, of sport and even of families, sadly. Were they to see a community of faith, worldwide in its appeal, multi-racial in its constitution, open to public gaze and totally committed to its message, yet completely united in mind and purpose, it would have the impact of a miraculous sign. And if that unity were born, first and foremost, of love, as the unity of the Father and the Son is, it would be doubly attractive.

I have seen people brought to faith in Christ because they have recognized that kind of unity in a particular congregation. Perhaps the day may come when many more will see it on the wider canvas of the world Church. Only then, I suppose, would this prayer of Jesus be fully answered.

In my own home, in my own church, is there this loving unity of heart and mind? If not, what steps could I take to co-operate with God in answering the prayer of Jesus?

THE GIFT OF GLORY

'The glory that you have given me I have given them, so that they may be one, as we are one, I in them and you in me, that they may become completely one, so that the world may know that you have sent me and have loved them even as you have loved me.'

JOHN 17:22–23

We have already encountered the word 'glory' several times, often in its past participle, 'glorified'. It is a great theme of John's Gospel, right from the Prologue, where the beloved disciple testifies that 'we have seen his [that is, the Word's] glory, the glory as of the Father's only Son, full of grace and truth' (1:14).

As the ministry of Jesus continued, he spoke often of the hour when he would be 'glorified' or 'enter into his glory'. On this very evening he told the disciples that that hour had now come, and that the promised Holy Spirit would glorify Jesus by 'taking what is mine and declaring it to you' (16:14).

Perhaps we can pause here to see how the entire Trinity is involved in this 'glory'. It is pre-eminently the glory of the Father revealed in his only Son. It is a glory to be declared by the Spirit. And it is the glory of Christ, which he had in the Father's presence 'before the world existed'. This is the glory of which Jesus 'emptied' himself by 'being born in human form' (Philippians 2:7) and it is the glory to which he will be restored when the final victory over sin and death has been accomplished.

Some glory! But what did Jesus say he had given his disciples? 'The glory that you have given me'! Can this possibly be true? That this bunch of fishermen, farmers and Galilean peasants, together with a reclaimed traitor to the Jewish cause, should have received the glory of the pre-existent Christ? That in some way they already shared in the triumph of the struggle that lay ahead, which at the moment seemed to them nothing but a terrifying prospect?

The language is quite unambiguous: 'I have given them the glory that you have given me.' But it is not, it would seem, unconditional. It is in some way tied in with the love and unity for which Jesus has been praying. It has been given 'so that they may be one, as we are one'. How can Christ's 'glory' help to bring about so desirable an end?

In the Prologue the glory of Jesus was described as 'full of grace and truth', so if his disciples had received his glory (perhaps the tense is the prophetic past, speaking of the future as though it had already happened) then they too would manifest 'grace and truth'. The grace and truth of God dwelt in Jesus ('as of the Father's only Son'), and now the grace and truth of Jesus were to dwell in his disciples. It is almost like a mathematical formula: God into Jesus *plus* Jesus into disciples *equals* a unity based on grace and truth. Indeed, Jesus prayed that it might be a complete, perfect, entire unity: 'that they may become *completely* one'. In that way they could demonstrate in their witness to the world the mystical reality of the love and unity which are the hallmarks of the Holy Trinity. And the world, which had found it so hard to 'believe' (v. 21), would then 'recognize' (the implication of the word 'know' here) that Jesus had been sent by God, for only a divine miracle could enable ordinary men and women to live in such unity and love.

Once again, all of this may sound like a complicated theological argument. In fact, it describes something which most Christians at some time in their lives have experienced, and that is the practical reality of such a loving unity. Because we are human, we often distort the beauty of our unity into dissension, envy and argument. But sometimes, as though at the touch of an angel's wing, we become aware of its presence—in a loving action, in a congregation's genuine love in some time of tragedy or disaster, in the enfolding arms of the fellowship when we feel otherwise isolated, lonely and afraid. So many people have said to me, 'I don't know how I would have got through it without the love and support of my church', and I have certainly known the experience myself. With all our faults, there is latent in the Christian *koinonia*, the fellowship, a love which goes beyond anything to be found elsewhere.

Such love is indeed only a mirror-image of the love of God and the love of Christ 'poured into our hearts by the Holy Spirit', but it is an image of the truth. It reflects a reality, not an illusion. It is the practical working-out in ordinary day-to-day living of the principles of grace and truth.

Grace and truth do not easily go together, because we often see 'truth' as something to be fought for or defended, and it is sometimes hard to do that with 'grace'. But as we have heard from the lips of Jesus in this discourse, *he* is 'the truth', not a series of propositions or doctrines. The 'Word', the revelation of God in Jesus, is 'the truth'. The Holy Spirit, and *only* the Holy Spirit, will 'lead us into all truth'. These are not battles to be fought, but revelations to be shared... yes, and as far as possible, to be shared with 'grace', that sense of undeserved blessing from the hands of God. In other words, 'truth' is not a stick with which to beat others, but a key with which we and they may unlock the purposes of God.

Interestingly, in practice few people are won for Christ by argument, but many more by gracious witness. Grace and truth can go hand in hand when they are being ministered by a people who know something of the loving unity of God. Such people will inevitably be like the ones Jesus prayed for here, who 'know that God has loved them even as he has loved the Son'. Knowing we are loved releases us to love.

Have I ever experienced that reality of Christian love which has such converting power? If I have, let me give thanks. If I have not yet done so, may I start by asking whether I recognize that I am loved by the Father and the Son and to what extent I recognize that same love in my fellow Christians.

TO SEE MY GLORY

'Father, I desire that those also, whom you have given me, may be with me where I am, to see my glory, which you have given me because you loved me before the foundation of the world.'

JOHN 17:24

We are always told that prayer is not about what we 'want' from God, but a collaboration with his will for us. Yet here Jesus quite evidently changed his prayer from 'asking' to 'wanting': 'Father, *I desire...*' However, there is no suggestion here of self-indulgence. The purposes of the Father and the Son are one, and so Jesus could confidently ask for what he desired, knowing that it would also be what the Father desired.

What he desired was actually something he had already promised his disciples, that they would one day be with him, to see his glory. Earlier that evening he had promised them, 'I will come again and take you to myself, so that where I am, there you may be also' (14:3). The 'extra' this time was the wish that they might see his 'glory', the gift of his Father's love 'before the foundation of the world'.

Once again we have this concept of 'glory'—not now the glory of the cross, nor even the empty tomb, but the glory of heaven itself. This prayer was the expression of the desire of Jesus that his earthly friends should one day see his heavenly glory, perhaps only then realizing to the full the extent of his own love for them. The word for 'see' here conveys the idea of rapt attention: their eyes would 'behold' the glory of Christ at the right hand of the Father in heaven.

I can remember as a choirboy long ago singing the lines of the hymn which speak of the 'rapture' of the Christian in heaven:

Prostrate before thy throne to lie
And gaze and gaze on thee.

Apart from the fact that I wasn't entirely sure what 'rapture' was, the whole idea didn't strike me as very attractive. Why would one wish to spend eons and eons of time lying flat on the ground gazing at the vision of God in heaven? Surely there would be something to *do*? In one sense I still reserve judgment on the Victorian hymn writer's view of heaven as a place of inactive adoration, but I think I can grasp something now of the wonder of discovery that will make what we call the beatific vision a source of deep joy and contentment—though I would add, with some relief, that Revelation also tells us that we shall 'serve' him—there will be 'something to *do*'!

But the vision will also serve to answer many questions and quieten many fears. For these disciples, for instance, the sight of the glory of Christ in heaven would put into perspective all the anxieties, trials, tribulations and persecution that they would suffer on earth. This is *not*—in the words of the old Communist jibe—'pie in the sky when you die'. Jesus never held heaven out to them as a compensation for earthly suffering, but as the eventual destination of the journey on which they were already travelling. But it would have been an enormous joy to Jesus to know that one day all their troubled questions would be answered and all their doubts resolved when they saw the fulfilment of God's great plan. However we are to conceive of heaven —and really, all the Bible gives us is pictures and visions—it will surely be the moment when we realize that the God we worship and have rather half-heartedly followed was right all along, that truth and justice will eventually prevail and that everything will be well.

What they would see, we notice, is 'my glory', rather than simply the glory of heaven. That would be of the greatest joy to them, to see the Saviour (in the words of the old hymn) 'vindicated, throned, adored'. Only then would they fully understand what Jesus had meant when he talked of his 'glorification' through the fulfilment of God's eternal purpose of love. It is the glory 'which you have given me because you loved me before the foundation of the world'.

This kind of language is unique to John's Gospel, which right from verse 1 sets the life and work of Jesus against a backdrop of eternity: 'In the beginning was the Word...' It implies that the Father–Son relationship, and indeed the relationship of the Father-Son to the Spirit, did not come into being simply to meet human need, but was an expression of the very nature of God. The God of the Bible, in other words, is not a simple unity but a complex relationship of Persons, a relationship which generates its own creative power. And right from the beginning this was a relationship of perfect love and unity.

Human beings are made in the 'image' of this Godhead. Most of our human joys and sorrows are caused by our relationships of one kind or another, and it is a wonderful consolation to understand that the God who made us is a God of relationship and also, in himself, an example of relationships which operate in constant harmony, unity of will, and love.

Out of that relationship of love and unity, Jesus came to earth. When John tells us in his first letter that 'the Father has sent his Son as the Saviour of the world' (4:14), we need to read it alongside his statement in this Gospel that 'God so *loved* the world that he gave his only Son' (3:16). The Father loved the Son, as we read in this very passage, but the Father also loved the world, and for love of the world he put the love of his Son to one side for a while. That is an instance of divine deprivation as well as a demonstration of the infinite love of God for what he had made. God was not prepared to stand by while the world destroyed itself. He cared for its people, men and women made in his own image, and for love of them was prepared to place his dearly beloved Son for a time into the hands of evil men.

That is true 'glory', the glory of self-giving love. That was the glory Jesus would show on the cross, in the darkness of that solemn noonday. But it was also the glory that one day his disciples (those then and those since) will one day see in the purer light of heaven.

Does heaven ever figure in my conscious thoughts? Does the promise of seeing Christ's glory mean anything to me in the ordinary rush and pressure of life? Is this because it is literally beyond comprehension? Or because it simply sounds too good to be true?

The triumph of love

'Righteous Father, the world does not know you, but I know you; and these know that you have sent me. I made your name known to them, and I will make it known, so that the love with which you have loved me may be in them, and I in them.'

JOHN 17:25–26

In the last part of this prayer Jesus has addressed his Father in three different ways, as 'Holy Father' (v. 11), as 'Father' (v. 24) and now as 'Righteous Father'. The three titles seem to have met three different circumstances. The first was in the context of prayer for the disciples in the unbelieving world, that they might be protected and kept 'holy'. The second was in the intimacy of prayer for his own particular friends. Now the third is set in the context of the cosmic struggle between truth and error and between good and evil into which the disciples were about to be launched.

This, the last petition of the high priestly prayer, is perhaps in some ways the most solemn of all, addressed to the 'Righteous' Father, the God of justice and judgment. After all, Jesus is seeking to make a mark of distinction between his disciples, who 'know that you have sent me', and the unbelieving world, which 'does not know you'.

So here, at the end of the evening, as at the beginning, 'knowing' is a constant theme. The world does not know God. That, in a word, is the world's problem—the failure to recognize the reality of its Creator. There is the failure that lies behind every other failure and every kind of sin. As we have seen, this lack of knowledge is much more than simple ignorance. This is a wilful refusal to see or recognize the truth.

How can we apply that to the world as we see it today? Are people culpable in their unbelief—deliberately and consciously *refusing* to believe? Or are some simply ignorant of the truth of God, or unconvinced by what they hear about him? Are some misled by the barrage of distortions and half-truths that saturate our society through the media? Are some victims of their own pride, which has led them to believe that the ultimate answers all lie in human cleverness and skill, and consequently can find no room in their thinking for the concept of a Creator-God?

It would be wrong to generalize. Some, undoubtedly, have been turned off the Christian message by an insensitive, crude or even misleading presentation of it. Some have never had that message presented to them in a way that they could understand or appreciate. Some have clung to bits and pieces of belief, aware in their inner beings of the reality of God but not able to relate that experience to the Christian story as a whole. Some have simply preferred the way of indulgence, setting self above spirit, and some have used their God-given intellects to reject the very notion of a Creator to whom they must give account. Just to list those examples (and there could be many more) will show how simplistic it is to talk of the 'world' as a coherent mass of God-rejecting unbelief.

Jesus recognized that fact in his own ministry, saying of a Roman centurion that he 'had not found such great faith even in Israel' (Luke 7:9)—although by normal criteria the man would have fallen well short of a coherent faith in God or Christ. The 'world', as Jesus used the word in this prayer, is clearly defined—not 'everybody', but secular society, however outwardly religious it might seem, organized to reject God, as it would reject Jesus the following day in his mockery of a trial.

That world did not know (recognize) God, and would not have accepted that Jesus knew him, either.

The disciples 'know that you have sent me'. That may not be quite the same as 'knowing God' but it is a vital step on the journey. They recognized that Jesus was from God and spoke with his authority. Step by step from that base they would eventually come to enter into a deeper knowledge of God, which would bring them into the full experience of his love and the continuing presence of Christ among them by the Holy Spirit. The whole purpose of Jesus in revealing the name (character) of the Father to them, and continuing to do so in the future, would be so that 'the love with which you have loved me may be in them, and I in them'.

That is the secret purpose of God, now revealed. Love will triumph—the love of the Father and the Son, manifested in the world by their witness. That truth makes a fitting end to Christ's prayer and a wonderful bridge into understanding the events that were now set in train as Jesus and the disciples entered 'a place where there was a garden' (18:1), the garden of the betrayal and arrest. In the end—lift up your hearts!—forgiveness of sins will be proclaimed to all the nations, and the world, apparently so set in its unbelief, will crumble before the claims of love.

Is it possible to draw a link between the washing of the disciples' feet, with which the Passover evening began, and the prayer that the world would eventually be won by the unity and love of the followers of Jesus, with which it closed?

'IT IS FINISHED'

When Jesus saw his mother and the disciple whom he loved stand-ing beside her, he said to his mother, 'Woman, here is your son.' Then he said to the disciple, 'Here is your mother.' And from that hour the disciple took her into his own home. After this, when Jesus knew that all was now finished, he said (in order to fulfill the scripture), 'I am thirsty.' A jar full of sour wine was standing there. So they put a sponge full of the wine on a branch of hyssop and held it to his mouth. When Jesus had received the wine, he said, 'It is finished.' Then he bowed his head and gave up his spirit.

JOHN 19:26–30

This is John's record of the awful happenings of Friday after-noon. Before then, but following the previous evening's meal and the discourse which has been our study through the last 37 days, had come the arrest of Jesus in the garden across the Kidron valley. That was followed by an examination by Annas, the father-in-law of the high priest Caiaphas, and then by Caiaphas himself, before, early on Friday morning, he was taken to the Roman Governor, Pilate. Although Pilate found 'no case against him' (18:38) he eventually, in response to the shouts of a crowd, delivered Jesus to be crucified.

There inevitably followed this sad and sombre scene. It was now that the women showed their devotion, most of the male disciples having scattered to avoid arrest. At the foot of the cross stood a small group of them—Mary (never referred to in this

Gospel by her name, but simply as 'the mother of Jesus'), her sister (Salome), and two other Marys, one 'the wife of Clopas' and the other Magdalene. The eyes of the dying Saviour lighted on his mother. One is irresistibly reminded of the Latin words of the Good Friday motet:

> *Stabat Mater dolorosa*
> *Dextra crucem, lacrimosa,*
> *Dum pendebat Filius.*

'The sorrowing Mother stood by the cross weeping, as they hanged her Son': could there be a more intense agony than to witness the child of her own body being slowly broken and killed before her eyes? Especially when she knew that his life had been dedicated to acts of mercy and love, that he was 'the Man for others'?

Jesus was moved by the sight of her, and from the cross itself made arrangements for her future care. Already, we must assume, a widow, and apparently having no other son to care for her (those described as 'brothers' of Jesus were probably in fact cousins) Mary was committed by Jesus to the care of the beloved disciple, who was also standing beside her. 'From that hour' he accepted the responsibility, and took her to his home until her death.

'After this'—the human duty of a son having been fulfilled— Jesus asked for a drink, which the watching soldiers provided on a sponge. When he had sipped it, Jesus raised his voice for one last cry. The other Evangelists record the strength of this final shout, but only the beloved disciple, perhaps, was in a position to hear what it was he cried out.

'It is *finished*'! The English word cannot quite convey the note of triumph. 'It is fully accomplished, it has been brought to completion, the responsibility has been discharged'... all are encompassed in the single word *tetelestai*. We have heard this word from the lips of Jesus before, in his prayer the previous evening: 'I have finished the work you gave me to do' (17:4). Now the sacrifice was complete. He could offer to the Father, on behalf of the world, a life of perfect love and obedience, knowing that through this act all that the Father had purposed would be achieved. This was not, in other words, a cry of defeat or despair, but of triumph.

That is not in any way to diminish the reality of his suffering on the cross, nor the cruelty and utter injustice of what had been done to him. The cross did not happen to tell us that the world is a good place, where all will be well, but to drive home the message that it is a place where sin is often dominant, and where only self-giving love can transform things. That was what was offered on Golgotha and that was what the Father accepted and through which blessing came to the whole world.

It might be possible to place ourselves into that sad scene around the cross. With whom can we most fully identify? The forgiven sinner, Mary Magdalene? The sorrowing mother, Mary? The friends and relatives who tried to give her support and sympathy? The beloved disciple, finding that in his great sorrow he was to be given a new responsibility? Although this looked like an ending, there were nevertheless the seeds here of the new life that was to come from the cross.

39

'THERE WAS A GARDEN'

Now there was a garden in the place where he was crucified, and in the garden there was a new tomb in which no one had ever been laid. And so, because it was the Jewish day of Preparation, and the tomb was nearby, they laid Jesus there.

JOHN 19:41–42

In the place where Jesus was crucified, there was a garden. What a paradox! In the place of death, there was a seedbed of life. In the place of cruelty and ugliness, there was a place of beauty. In the place of tears and suffering, there was a place of rest and joy.

Gardens occur at strategic points throughout the Bible's story, but three of them seem particularly relevant to our study. The first garden was the Garden of Eden, the place of beauty and delight, where the first man tended the profusion of flowers, shrubs and trees that filled it with fruit for the taste, scent for the nose and colour for the eye. It was in Eden, so the story tells us, that man was given his companion and partner, Eve, and life was tranquil and serene.

But it was also Eden that was the scene of the first and tragic sin, the wilful disobedience that cost the man and the woman their blissful dwelling place. That sin was not, as some seem to think, simply to 'eat an apple'; nor was it, as others suppose, something to do with sex. It was simply the most basic of all sins—thinking that they knew better than God what was good for them.

That has been the root of all subsequent sin, and could be seen as the cause of all our troubles. We, in our folly and pride, think we know better than our Creator. That was the sin that has blighted the human race all through its history, and still does today. Disobedience to God's will simply means that we prefer ours to his. The consequences, individually and socially, have been disastrous.

That brings us to the second garden, the garden of Gethsemane. There the will of the Son of God submitted—not without a struggle, not without tears—to the will of the Father. It cost probably more than we shall ever know for Jesus to say, on the eve of a hideous and painful execution, 'Not my will but yours be done' (Luke 22:42). Yet in that single act of obedience he was to open the way for the forgiveness of all our disobediences.

But it was not simply an act of stern duty. It was in love for the lost that God sent his Son into the world. It was, Jesus said, 'to seek out and to save the lost' that he had come (Luke 19:10). It was not cold duty but the passionate love of God for his stumbling and rebellious creatures that drew Jesus to the cross. The battle was settled by that act of sublime submission. All that followed—the arrest, the trial, the scourging, the nails and the sword-wound—were its inevitable consequence. It was in the garden of Gethsemane, in the cool of an April evening, under the ancient olive trees, that the decisive struggle for our salvation took place.

And now there was the garden of the Tomb, which during the night that was to follow became the garden of the Resurrection. In a place where seeds are planted and new life constantly springs forth, the body of the world's Saviour was 'planted', and from his death sprung forth a wonderful harvest of eternal life.

It was for the length of a Sabbath that Jesus rested there in the sleep of death. It seems appropriate that the one interlude, as it were, in this dramatic narrative took place on the day God had appointed a rest for all his people.

This is a time to pause and reflect. The light of the world has been put out, for the moment. It might seem that darkness has triumphed, even though we are told by John that 'the darkness did not overcome it' (1:5). But the seed of eternal life is germinating within the stone-locked tomb.

40

CALLED AND SENT

When it was evening on that day, the first day of the week, and the doors of the house where the disciples had met were locked for fear of the Jews, Jesus came and stood among them and said, 'Peace be with you.' After he said this, he showed them his hands and his side. Then the disciples rejoiced when they saw the Lord. Jesus said to them again, 'Peace be with you. As the Father has sent me, so I send you.'

JOHN 20:19–21

It was, we may assume, the same house and the same upper room, and only three evenings after these same disciples had sat in awe as their master told them what was to happen. On Thursday evening their hearts were 'troubled', made anxious by the words of Jesus and the thought that he was about to leave them. On this night, that sense of unease had grown into a fear approaching terror. They had seen what the authorities had done to their leader, a man so powerful and strong. What kind of fate might be visited on his miserable and bereft followers?

So the 'doors were locked for fear of the Jews'—presumably the Jewish authorities, for everyone inside the room was also Jewish! Their anxiety may have been increased by what Mary Magdalene had so recently told them, with her claim that she had 'seen the Lord' (20:18), and also the testimony of Peter and the beloved disciple of what they had discovered at the tomb of Jesus (20:3–9).

It is hard to imagine, therefore, what emotions must have flooded into their startled minds as a figure appeared in the room, locked doors notwithstanding. Their eyes told them that it was Jesus, but their reason argued against it. Was this a ghost, sent to terrify them? It was perhaps as well that the figure's first words were familiar ones—'Peace be with you', presumably *Shalom* in Hebrew. He then showed them 'his hands and his side', the visible, if cruel, evidences that this really was Jesus and these truly were the marks of his suffering two days earlier.

Perhaps it was the sight of those scars, at once terrible and glorious, that set them free to believe that their master was standing there before them and that his repeated promise that 'on the third day' he would rise again had been fulfilled. At any rate, '*then* the disciples rejoiced'. Like Mary Magdalene, they had 'seen the Lord'.

Again Jesus spoke his word of reassurance: 'Peace be with you'. But he followed it with a command, one which complemented precisely both the promise and the commission he had shared with them on that Thursday evening: 'As the Father has sent me, so I send you.'

In his high priestly prayer Jesus had spoken of this double commission, his own and theirs. 'As you have sent me into the world,' he had prayed to the Father, 'so I have sent them into the world.' In fact, Jesus spoke on that evening as though the prophecy were already fulfilled. Now it is nearer that fulfilment, though the sending out itself would wait for another forty days, until the feast of Pentecost. Then, in the promised gift of the divine Helper, the Holy Spirit, the disciples were finally sent out as Christ's witnesses 'in Jerusalem, in all Judea and Samaria, and to the ends of the earth' (Acts 1:8).

But it was the one who was sent who did the sending! The Father sent the Son, and in the fullness of time the Son sent the disciples—the Twelve, at first, but then the whole company of the believers. As Luke tells us, 'Those who were scattered went from place to place, proclaiming the word' (Acts 8:4)—and these are identified as all the disciples *except* the apostles (8:1). All were called, all were forgiven, all received the gift of the Holy Spirit and *all were sent out*. The Anglican Communion service does well to call those who have received the comfort of the sacrament to receive also this divine commission: 'Send us out in the power of your Spirit to live and work to your praise and glory.' We are a missionary people, because we serve a missionary God, who sent his Son, who in turn now sends us.

This little scene in the upper room is really the epilogue to all that was said on the Thursday evening. As Jesus had promised, he had gone away, and their hearts had been sad, but now they had seen him again and are rejoicing. There would be one more 'leaving', on the mount of the Ascension, and one more 'coming', again in this same upper room (Acts 1:13), when the promised Spirit would bring Jesus to them in a new way. The story would then be complete, except that in one sense it will never be complete until that day when 'the earth is full of the knowledge of the Lord' and every tongue confesses that 'Jesus Christ is Lord, to the glory of God the Father' (Isaiah 11:9; Philippians 2:11).

For further reading

Readings in St John's Gospel, William Temple, Macmillan, 1961.
(I have made several references to Temple's classic
devotional commentary on John. There are a number of
different editions available for the present-day reader.)

John, Richard A. Burridge, The People's Bible Commentary,
BRF, 1998.

The Priority of John, John A.T. Robinson, SCM Press, 1985.

DISCUSSION STARTERS

Some people will doubtless wish to use this book as a basis for
Lent discussion or reflection groups. While each day's reading
has some thoughts for reflection, especially for the individual
reader, and these may provide ideas for a group, here are
suggestions for six weekly sessions based around the book.

SESSION ONE

THE FAITH JOURNEY

Key passage: John 14:1–6
The upper room discourses, and therefore this passage, are
preceded by the incident of the foot-washing (13:1–15). If your
group are willing and eager, it might be an idea to start your first
session with a buffet meal together, preceded by a simple
ceremony in which you all wash each other's feet! Then the
words of Jesus from 13:12–15 could be read aloud.

However, the passage under reflection comes after the supper
and after Jesus had told them that where he was going they
could not come at present (13:33, 36), so it is in the context
of *loss*. That is why their hearts were 'troubled'. So the passage

is very relevant to those who are experiencing loss, especially bereavement, and that could well be the main topic of consideration. Some of the questions it raises are:

- How do we relate the idea of 'travel lodges' on the journey beyond death to our understanding of 'heaven'? Do people find the idea of the 'journey' a helpful one? Does this passage have a particular resonance for those who have recently been bereaved?

- Considering verse 6, how do the group members apply this statement to our understanding of 'other faiths'? How do people react to the quotation from Richard Burridge? You might like to refer to Paul's teaching in Romans 2:12–16.

- Do group members find the ideas of 'way' (journey), 'truth' (belief) and 'life' (spiritual energy and strength) helpful as pictures of Christian discipleship? Some might like to relate them to their own experience of the journey of faith.

ASKING IN HIS NAME

Key passage: John 14:12–18
'If in my name you ask me for anything, I will do it.' That apparently blanket promise might make a good start to a discussion! What are the group members' experiences of answered or 'unanswered' prayer? Have there been times when they have prayed and felt convinced their prayer would be answered, only to be disappointed?

The questions this passage might raise are:

- What are the 'greater works' that the followers of Jesus would be able to do after he has left them (and the Helper has come)? Does verse 13 suggest parameters to the promise of verse 14, and if so, what are they? How do we understand 'in my name' and 'so that the Father may be glorified'?

• Looking back at verses 8–11, do they help us to clarify the way we think of Jesus in relation to his Father? Is it true that most people find it easier to think in terms of Jesus than the Father? Is that our own experience? Is there any danger that we might end up with a 'Jesus religion' rather than a Trinitarian one? How do we think of God showing us himself 'through' Jesus?

THE HELPER AND ADVOCATE

Key passage: John 14:25–27

It might be an idea to go round the group and invite people to say how they think of the Holy Spirit. There might be some strange answers! Do they find the language of this passage more helpful—the Spirit as Teacher, Reminder, Advocate (pleading our case) and Strengthener? Is the all-embracing title 'Helper' a way to think of the Holy Spirit? Or do people respond better to the idea of the Spirit as simply the presence of Jesus with his people?

Possible questions for discussion might be:

• If Jesus promised the Holy Spirit to the Church, and assuming he has kept his promise, what do we think ought to be the evidences of his presence?

• The early Church experienced the Holy Spirit in very visible ways—speaking in tongues, prophecy, miracles of healing and so on. Some Christians would say that the problem with today's Church is that these 'gifts of the Spirit' have been ignored or even refused. How do group members react to that? Have any members of the group personal experiences to share?

- Paul teaches that the chief evidence of the Spirit's work is the 'fruit of the Spirit' (see Galatians 5:22–24). It might be interesting to look up this passage and ask ourselves how evident this fruit is in our own churches.

THE VINE

Key passage: John 15:1–8

This discussion should appeal to gardeners! In fact, it might be an idea to get one or two members to explain the principle of pruning in order to get more fruit, and also the way in which the nutrients in the soil reach the branches and then the fruit through the trunk.

Questions that might arise include:

- If the vine is Jesus Christ and his disciples are branches 'in him', what would it mean for his Father to 'prune' one of those branches? Doesn't that sound a bit drastic? How does this image relate to the words of Jesus in the other Gospels that his disciples will be 'known by their fruit' (see Matthew 7:17–20)? Does it mean that a 'fruitless' disciple is to be 'cut off'? Or is it simply that a fruitless disciple is as useless as a dead branch?

- What does it mean to 'remain in' Christ? In practical terms, how would we do this? Are there dangers in getting 'separated' from him? Have any of the group personal experience of that?

THE PARTING GIFT

Key passage: John 16:8–16
As people often have difficulty in grasping the concept of the Holy Spirit, or at any rate putting it into words, it might be an idea to invite members of the group to share their own feelings, ideas and experiences (if any) of the third member of the Trinity.

The various words that can be used to translate the title 'Paraclete' may offer a basis for discussion. Do some think of him as 'Guide'? Or 'Helper'? Or 'Advocate', arguing their cause? Or Comforter, Teacher, even Accuser? Perhaps the most helpful direction to take is to concentrate on the Spirit as Jesus both 'with' and 'in' (or 'among') his people.

The evening might conclude with a simple time of prayer invoking the presence and help of the Holy Spirit in our own lives. The *Veni Creator* ('Come, Holy Ghost, our souls inspire…') might make a suitable prayer for the group quietly to join in at the end.

CHRISTIANS AND THE 'WORLD'

Key passage: John 17:13–21
Many people are confused by the fourth Gospel's attitude to the 'world'. After all, they say, is not the world, the *cosmos*, created by God and declared by him to be 'very good' (Genesis 1:31)? So why should Christians be enjoined to 'hate' the world and reject it? Wouldn't that logically mean that we should all enter

monasteries or isolate ourselves from the lives of other people?

It is important to understand the special way in which John uses this word. For him, the 'world' is human society organized as though God didn't exist—hence, intrinsically evil and to be rejected. The group might like to study carefully the words of Jesus in this chapter, where they will see that he did not want his followers to abandon the world but to be his witnesses within it, so that 'the world might believe'. In other words, Jesus has not abandoned the world or given up hope for it!

It might be a good area of discussion to consider the way in which our ordinary life in 'the world'—in the home, at work, among friends, neighbours and communities—relates to our life of faith. Are there tensions, contradictions, points where they seem to pull in opposite directions? How, then, can we fulfil Christ's prayer that we should be 'in' the world, but not 'of' it?

www.brf.org.uk

Enter an author, title, subject or phrase

Books ○
Extracts/Info ◉

go

brf

Barnabas

Resourcing your spiritual journey

Home
Bible Centre
Book news
Events
Articles
Authors
Who is BRF?

The Bible Reading Fellowship
First Floor
Elsfield Hall
15–17 Elsfield Way
Oxford
OX2 8FG
England
Tel 01865 319700
Fax 01865 319701
E-mail
enquiries@brf.org.uk

Welcome to BRF

For Bible based resources and information for today's Christian living and for details of all BRF publications, extracts and articles, and a wealth of other information.

Find out about:

■ New BRF publications

■ BRF's comprehensive range of resources:
  Bible reading and study; Prayer and spirituality; Lent and Advent

■ BRF authors

■ Quiet days, Retreats and other events

■ Barnabas (storybooks, seasonal activity books and teaching resources for 3–11 year olds)

■ The Barnabas Live Creative Arts and Schools Programme

Visit the BRF website at www.brf.org.uk

BRF is a Registered Charity